Only Visiting This Planet

ONLY VISITING THIS PLANET

Text by Nigel Suckling

Foreword by Arthur C. Clarke

FOR JEAN, TONY AND TERRY

Page 1 SCORPIUS 1988
GOUACHE AND INK. 6.7 x 7.4 IN. (17 x 9CM). Cover illustration, Coronet Books.
This emblem for a James Bond story by John Gardner was based on a very rough sketch by
the art director, which Danny had to decipher and complete in a weekend.

Page 2 TORTOISESHELLS 1992
GOUACHE AND INK. 13.3 x 19.6 IN. (34 x 50CM). Private work.
This is one of the pictures Danny exhibited at the Minehead Space Festival in 1992, which
he was invited to by Arthur C. Clarke. It was painted for his own amusement, but was
spotted at the exhibition by a gentleman who bought it for his living room wall.

An imprint of Dragon's World
Limpsfield
Surrey RH8 0DY
Great Britain

First published by Dragon's World 1994

© Dragon's World 1994
© Illustrations: Danny Flynn 1994
© Text: Nigel Suckling 1994

All rights reserved

EDITOR: Fiona Trent
DESIGN AND TYPESETTING: Bob Gordon Design
EDITORIAL DIRECTOR: Pippa Rubinstein
ART DIRECTOR: John Strange

The catalogue record for this book is available from the British Library

ISBN 1 85028 267 6

Printed in Singapore

CONTENTS

THE OCEA

FOREWORD BY

ARTHUR C. CLARKE

THE OCEAN 1992
GOUACHE AND INK.
14.5 x 19.6 IN. (37 x 50CM).
Illustration for the Boots 1994
calendar. 'Annoyingly the original
artwork has been "lost", which is a
pity as it was going to be a
Christmas present for my Dad. He'll
have to settle for some socks this
year instead.'

SCIENCE FICTION AND FANTASY have inspired enormous quantities of art: good, bad, indifferent and brilliant. If, as many believe, this is the Golden Age of Science Fiction, it may well be the Golden Age of Science Fiction Art, and I'm delighted to see this collection of Danny Flynn's work. He has the ability to blend real objects into imaginary landscapes, evoking the 'sense of wonder' which is really at the heart of all good Science Fiction and Fantasy. (No, I'm not going to get involved in that tedious debate: I've settled it once and for all with Clarke's diktat 'Science Fiction is something that could happen, though you'd often be sorry if it did: Fantasy couldn't happen, though you often wish it could.'

I would like to pay a brief tribute to some of the artists whose work I have enjoyed in this field – going all the way back to the now almost forgotten S.H. Sime, who illustrated many of Lord Dunsany's books (I still have several volumes signed by them both). Later, Virgil Finley followed the tradition with a very similar technique.

And then of course, there was the great Frank R. Paul – probably regarded with a tolerant smile by today's critics. But for the late 1920s, and early 30s, his garish poster-colours were just what the doctor (and Hugo Gernsbach) ordered. Although all his human characters look the same, the scope of his imagination for extraterrestrials and interplanetary landscapes may still be unsurpassed.

I suppose Chesley Bonestell is still the most famous of all artists in this field – and more than that, his gorgeous paintings, later collected in the Conquest of Space played an important role in the genesis of the forthcoming Space Age. Many of today's astronauts and aerospace engineers must have been inspired by his almost photographically realistic images of the Moon, Mars and, above all, Saturn and its glorious rings, dominating the sky of its nearer moons.

It would be invidious to mention any of today's practising artists, though I'm tempted to do so, as I have met many of them and several have illustrated my own books. But I cannot forbear to mention the two friends, who have unique status because they have been there, and have come back to paint what they have seen. I refer, of course, to cosmonaut Alexei Leonov and astronaut Alan Bean – the first real space artists. In fact, Alan is now a full-time artist, and I believe doing quite well in his new profession.

But back to Danny – I hope you will enjoy his volume and feel that, thanks to him, you are indeed looking through 'charmed magic casements, opening on the foam, of perilous seas in faery lands folorn.'

ARTHUR C. CLARKE
COLOMBO, SRI LANKA
17TH MAY 1993

CRYSTAL SWORD 1988
GOUACHE AND INK. 11.4 x 16.9 IN. (29 x 43CM).
Cover for a book by Adrienne Martine-Barnes, Headline Press. The second in a series of four books by this author, the story being set in an alternative Britain of the dim and distant past. The swords featured on all four covers were inspired by some of those that adorn the walls of the Black Prince pub in Woodstock near Oxford, where incidentally, there is also a knight in armour standing at the bar.

▲ **DOUBLE DRAGON 111 1991**
GOUACHE AND INK. 13.7 x 19.6 IN. (35 x 50CM).
Computer game box cover, Camel Advertising. An 'emergency' illustration that was required at very short notice. Danny was a bit surprised to see the Kung Fu fighters in the finished picture as he has no memory of having painted them. Sadly, the artwork was ruined in a flash flood that struck Camel's Sheffield office, taking with it over a thousand paintings.

▲ **PENNY ROYAL 1989**
GOUACHE AND INK.
8.2 x 14.5 IN. (21 x 37CM).
Cover for a mystery novel by Susan Moody, Futura Books. Danny had only a synopsis of the story to work from, but from it managed to work all the major clues into the picture.

▶ **SCAVENGER 1989**
GOUACHE AND INK.
12.2 x 18.5 IN. (31 x 47CM).
Computer game box cover, Hewson Games. This game involves a character who is repeatedly trapped in different cultures and in different periods of history and has to find ways of returning to the present day – hence the presence of the red telephone box. Problems with the software meant that the project was cancelled at the last moment.

◀ **DREAM YEARS 1985**
GOUACHE AND INK.
12.3 x 16.9 IN. (32 x 43CM).
Cover for a book by Lisa Goldstein, Allen & Unwin. One of Danny's earliest commissions and his first wraparound cover. To represent past, present and future he had what seemed to be a clever idea of showing three different clocks, but when the proof arrived he discovered he had failed to allow for the bar code, which completely obliterated one of them, rather undermining the concept.

CHAPTER ONE

PASTORAL FANTASY

PEREGRINE 1993
GOUACHE AND INK.
13 x 20.4 IN. (33 x 52CM).
Private work.

THE INTERVIEWS FOR THIS BOOK STARTED on a propitious note. While driving into Oxford after the preliminary interrogation, Danny glanced sideways through the car window and spotted three puppies in a field below his house. Not just any puppies, but three of a friend's Border Collie's puppies which had escaped the week before, evaded all search parties and sadly, been assumed to have ended up on some fox's dinner plate. But there they were playing on the edge of an island of greenery beneath an electricity pylon amidst a sea of mud that was a ploughed field after a week of heavy rain.

Some rapid backtracking and a slithering ride in the neighbour's Land Rover later, the three were rescued and returned to their pen – distinctly thinner and smaller than their stay-at-home siblings, and with ravenous appetites, but otherwise none the worse for their adventure.

Danny lives in a stone and brick farmhouse split into two cottages and perched high on a hillside between fields and some woodland rich in wildlife. Although only five or ten minutes drive from Oxford, the place has a remote feel. There are no other houses nearby and it is reached by a long dirt track overlooked by his studio, which Danny finds useful when deciding whether to be in or not to callers.

The Oxford area (and indeed one or other half of the building which is his current home) has been his base for several years. He moved there from London to live with a girlfriend with whom he had been conducting a long distance affair. Sadly, the relationship did not last – at least partly because of the weird hours they both worked, she was a nurse while he had an illustrator's notorious deadlines to meet. But another relationship followed and by the time that reached a conclusion he felt no urge to leave the area.

Danny Flynn was born on 8 September 1958 and grew up in Scunthorpe in Lincolnshire, of which he retains many vivid early memories including the last British Rail steam engines. The Celtic ring to his name comes from his father who hails from Kerry in south west Ireland. Danny has visited Eire a few times, and feels another trip is long overdue, but his roots are firmly in the north of England in general and Scunthorpe in particular.

Danny traces the earliest stirrings of an interest in art to the cards he collected from boxes of teabags from about the age of five years onwards – cards which came in series about fish, butterflies, ships, flags and so on. He was particularly attracted to the nature cards, and his father encouraged this interest by getting him to learn the names of all the creatures featured. Soon he was getting crayons and sketchpads for Christmas and he promptly filled them with drawings of wildlife, copying unashamedly from the cards and a growing collection of natural history books on the principle that most wild creatures will not sit still long enough for a decent picture to be made of them. In addition, he began copying his favourite comic characters and started to experiment with colour. He recalls using 'those giant paintboxes that had hundreds of colours and a useless brush in the middle, always with a cowboy or circus scene on the lid. I could never lift the lid without feeling compelled to add a drop of water to every little coloured square staring up at me.'

Fantasy did not really appeal to Danny as a subject for art till he was about ten years old when his imagination was sparked by free gift models in breakfast cereal packets. The models called, almost certainly, Krater Kreechurs, were a set of eight imaginary aliens about two inches (five centimetres) tall that came in fluorescent colours. They were part of the mania for anything remotely to do with space, which was prompted by the Apollo moon landing of the time. Although he can remember the creatures in almost perfect detail, including their names, Danny has occasionally wondered if he

▶ **WATERFALL 1993**
GOUACHE AND INK.
13.3 × 19.6 IN. (34 × 50CM).
Private work. Images and ideas frequently just spring into Danny's mind; he always jots them down in the hope of returning to them when time allows. This is one such picture, which he felt just had to be completed. Danny feels it is a good example of the direction in which his work is currently moving.

dreamed them because he has yet to meet anyone else with the faintest recollection of the things.

He had earlier been a fan of such children's SF shows on television as *Dr Who*, *Lost in Space* and *Thunderbirds*, and had even won a Stingray hat in a colouring competition in the magazine *TV21*. But somehow, his drawing imagination did not really take to the subject till the Krater Kreechurs came along – after which he began churning out hundreds of his own designs of aliens. Fantasy (in the broadest sense) soon came to equal nature as a favourite subject for pictures. To this day he enjoys both lines of work and to an extent they feed off each other. Certainly, Danny's fantasy work is greatly enriched by his fascination with nature, while in some of his straight nature scenes one would not be surprised if elves and goblins suddenly emerged from the undergrowth.

At junior school Danny was encouraged to paint by his teacher, Mrs McCowen; 'It's only when looking back that you realize the value of such people. At my first school I was quite introverted but art drew me out of myself and gave me a great lift. We're still friends now.'

Danny found it useful being known to have a talent for something at school. In his case it was not only art but also football, which he grew passionately fond of in the glory days of George Best at Manchester United: 'If you were good at something it gained you a certain respect that kept you out of fights and other trouble. Luckily, I had a reputation for both drawing and football so I had a relatively easy and enjoyable time.

In secondary school Danny's interest in art was further encouraged by his art teacher; he was young, and felt more like an older brother to Danny than a teacher. 'If it wasn't for him I don't think I would ever have become an illustrator. I don't know if it's still true, but when I was at school art was not highly regarded as a subject. And if you were in a high-grade class it was considered a waste of time, which was a terrible attitude, because it meant children like me could be pressurized into taking the wrong track.'

▶ **METAMORPHOSIS 1984**
GOUACHE AND INK.
11 x 16.5 IN. (28 x 42CM).
College work inspired by a Michael Moorcock novel. This was the last painting Danny produced at college, the last also of a group based on Moorcock's *Dancers at the End of Time*. Since there was a deadline for the project – it had to be completed in four days – Danny severely restricted the range of the colours used. Curiously, this was the most popular painting of the set and has continued to earn praise ever since.

▼ **PAINTED LADY ON ROSE 1987**
GOUACHE AND INK.
3.9 x 5.5 IN. (10 x 14CM).
Cassette cover, New World Cassettes. This image was also used as a greetings card to promote the Blenheim Palace Butterfly House.

However, with the right encouragement he persevered and after school enrolled on an art foundation course, for which he had to commute daily to Grimsby, some thirty miles (forty-eight kilometres) away. The travelling was not an enjoyable experience, since the only morning train got him to college an hour before it opened. Without his mother to turf him out of bed in the mornings he doubts that he would have completed the course. The college itself was fine and Danny's head of department is recalled with particular fondness. When confronted with the vandalism of one of his more rebellious punk students – a massive reclining nude on a public wall – the head agreed it was indeed a sad case, the quality of the artwork was well below the student's usual standard.

What were Danny's art interests at the time? 'When considering the classic artists it was basically anything weird and strange from Bosch to Salvador Dali, and particularly Magritte. That seems odd now, rather narrow, because these days I enjoy all kinds of art. Going to Kingston Art College later broadened my horizons.' He had also long admired Roger Dean's work on record covers for bands such as Yes and Osibisa, and while on the foundation course he discovered Dean's book *Views*. The book so fired his imagination that as he perused it on the way home on the bus, he almost missed his stop.

Danny's year at Grimsby coincided with the punk revolution, and because of the strong ties then between fantasy art and rock music he found himself at odds with many of his peers. Much of his favourite music in his teens, for example, David Bowie, Led Zeppelin, Pink Floyd, Yes and especially Tangerine Dream, was scorned by punks and Danny found the art he was interested in doing also being dismissed as hippy vapouring. So he was unsure about the punk movement and did not appreciate the music until the second wave of bands came along, bands such as Police, the Undertones and the Boomtown Rats. Fortunately, his interest in these bands did not require him to reappraise his values, or his musical taste, completely.

One of the greatest inspirations for Danny on a personal level was an old man he met through a Sunday paper round. Part of the job was to collect money from the customers and Danny was distinctly nervous about approaching this apparently eccentric old man in his studio. Mr Knight (as he was respectfully known) turned out to be a wonderful person, a railwayman who had taken up painting on retirement and discovered a vocation. Danny recalls him saying, 'I haven't wasted my life Danny, but I've only just come into my own. I wish I'd done this sooner. I never get ill now and I can't die yet, there's too much work to do first.' They became great friends and in fact, Mr Knight lived into his nineties, at which time he had a touching habit of referring to his son, then in his seventies, as 'my little boy'.

▶ **BLUEBELL WOODS 1992**
GOUACHE AND INK.
11.8 x 17.2 IN. (30 x 45CM).
Limited edition print. The scene is of some woods just five minutes walk from Danny's home and where he often goes when he wants to be alone or has something to think about, such as an idea for a book cover. He has done several versions of the picture. This is the definitive one undertaken after its success as a greeting card. Close inspection reveals an owl, a toad, three rabbits and four pixies which were, of course, painted straight from life.

▼ **REDWALL 1987**
GOUACHE AND INK.
5.1 x 5.1 IN. (13 x 13CM).
Unpublished cover illustration, Arrow Books. This was commissioned for the paperback edition of the Brian Jacques novel, but the publishers decided at the last minute to use the hardback cover instead. 'A shame for me' says Danny, 'as I thoroughly enjoyed the book and rate it even more highly than *Watership Down*.'

▶ **KINGFISHER 1991**

GOUACHE AND INK.
12.5 x 19.6 IN. (32 x 50CM).
Private work. This began life as a
sample painting, a new version of a
cover for some music entitled *Peace*
published by New World Cassettes.
When it was half completed on his
drawing board, Danny's father took
a liking to it and so was given the
final version for Christmas.

▲ **STAGS 1992**

GOUACHE AND INK. 12.5 x 17.7 IN. (32 x 45CM).

Private work. A lone stag looks bemusedly on as two stag beetles battle it out in this otherwise serene setting. The picture was prompted by the memory of cycling home one balmy summer evening and riding straight into a flying stag beetle: 'It was like being hit by a stone – the impact split my head open, the beetle, however, just picked itself up and walked away as if nothing had happened.'

▶ **PUFFIN 1993**

GOUACHE AND INK. 11.8 x 17.7 IN. (30 x 45CM).

Private work. Part of a personal project in which familiar creatures are placed in unlikely settings. 'Puffins look strange enough when seen in their natural environment,' Danny comments, 'so I was curious to see if they looked even stranger in an alien landscape.'

◄ **ALLSORTS 1993**
GOUACHE AND INK. 9.05 x 14.1 IN. (23 x 36CM).
Private work. This and the picture above were inspired by
one of Danny's particularly strange dreams. The
ladybirds, which appear to be seeping from one picture
into the other, remind him of a plague of ladybirds that
descended on Scunthorpe in 1977. It was the year of the
great British drought, and, as Danny recalls, 'they
covered everything like candyfloss and had literally to be
shovelled out of driveways.'

▲ **TREE-GIRL 1993**
GOUACHE AND INK. 9.05 x 14.1 IN. (23 x 36CM).
Private work. In Danny's local wood, Higgin's Wood, there
is a tree with an almost girl-like shape that he used to
form the basis of this composition. On the day he started
this piece Danny won two goldfish at St Giles Fair, and
somehow, they seemed to fit the scene.

▲ **ILLUSTRATED MAN 1993**
GOUACHE AND INK.
11.02 x 17.3 IN. (28 x 44CM).
Private work. Based on the opening story of
Ray Bradbury's *The Veldt*, the painting
features a futuristic mural in a children's
bedroom, which, complete with sounds and
smells, takes on a mysterious life of its own.
The picture began life as a college project
and was later reworked during a quiet spell.

▶ **BEE-EATER 1993**
GOUACHE AND INK. 12.5 x 18.1 IN. (32 x 46CM).
Private work. The original version of this picture was undertaken as a
therapeutic exercise after Danny survived a nasty car crash in May
1987. The crash happened at night so it was not till they returned in
daylight that they realized there could be a problem in finding a yellow
car in a field of oil-seed rape. The painting was done left-handed, as
Danny's normal painting hand had the shakes. The completed picture
was eventually used for the cover of a New World music cassette
entitled, ironically, *Journey*.

▶ **TOPIARY GARDENS 1992**
GOUACHE AND INK.
7.4 x 11.02 IN. (19 x 28CM).
Private work.

▶ **THE SQUONK 1993**
GOUACHE AND INK.
13.7 x 18.9 IN. (35 x 48CM).
Private work. Inspired by the song of
the same title on the Genesis album
Trick of the Tail. This refers to a
story of a creature that used to hide
in the woods and sob to itself
because it was so ugly. Eventually,
it was captured, put in a sack and
taken to the local king. When the
sack was opened they found the
Squonk had dissolved, literally, into
a pool of tears. The setting for the
painting is Danny's local woodland
and he surrounded the Squonk with
other ugly creatures in an attempt to
make him feel better.

When he was three or four Danny
acquired an invisible friend – an
imaginary living toy called Juju, a
name he conjured up without having
heard it used as a term for magic.
Although he cannot draw or describe
it now beyond calling it a 'greeny
squat thing', he could visualize it
perfectly at the time. When he
moved at the age of five the
creature sadly vanished, but
perhaps this Squonk is a partial
reincarnation.

► **TOPIARY COTTAGE 1992**
GOUACHE AND INK.
7.4 x 11.02 IN. (19 x 28CM).
Private work.

► **PEACOCK LADY 1993**
GOUACHE AND INK.
9.8 x 14.1 IN. (25 x 36CM).
Private work. The four pictures on
this spread are taken from an
ongoing personal project of Danny's
titled, provisionally, *The Peacock and
the Pixies*. It is a children's story with
a gentle environmental message
inspired by one of his favourite pubs,
the Trout near Oxford, an idyllic place
by a stream where peacocks roam
the gardens. Danny has long been
fascinated by peacocks, both the bird
and butterfly varieties, so it is an
ideal theme to concentrate on. The
story is still incomplete, but all it
needs, he believes, is three or four
months free from other distractions
to complete the work.

◄ **CAMBERWELL BEAUTY 1993**
GOUACHE AND INK.
10.6 x 14.5 IN. (27 x 37CM).
Private work. A less detailed version of
this picture was used as a greetings card
by the Blenheim Palace Butterfly House.
After hearing it praised on the air by the
DJ Bob Harris, Danny sent him the
original and felt inspired to tackle the
theme again.

▲ **WHALE KILLER 1993**
GOUACHE AND INK. 8.6 x 11.8 IN. (22 x 30CM).
Private work. The question posed by this picture is whether
the bird is enormous or the whale tiny. Danny himself is not
totally sure, but inclines towards the latter. He has always
been fascinated by bonsai trees and, if some biological
equivalent were available (which with current trends in genetic
engineering is not all that far fetched), he would love to have
a goldfish bowl in his living room with miniature whales
swimming around in it.

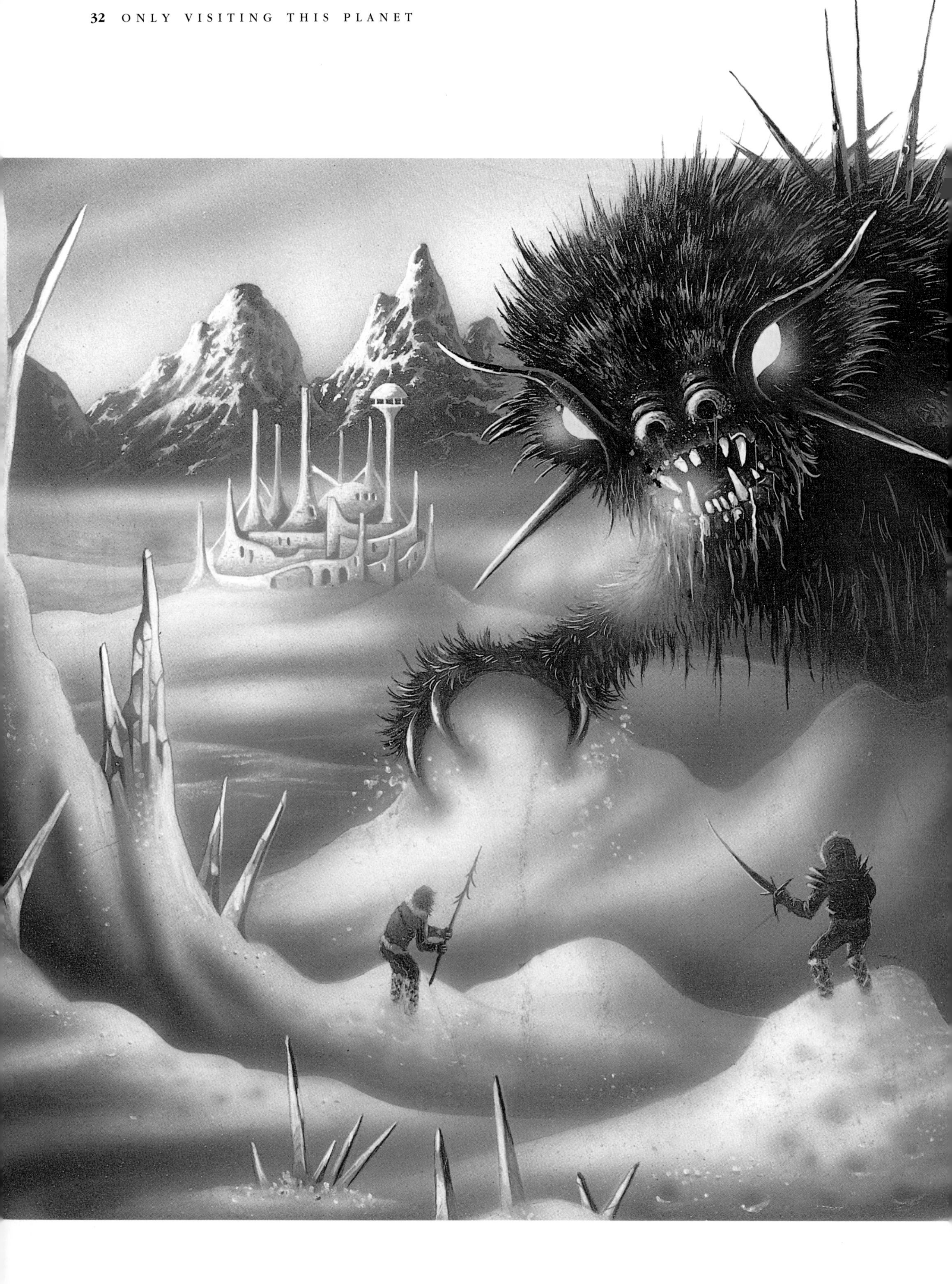

CHAPTER TWO

SWORD AND SORCERY

BLOODSWORD V: THE WALLS OF SPYTE 1988
GOUACHE AND INK. 8.2 x 12.5 IN. (21 x 32CM).
Cover for a book by Dave Morris and Oliver Johnson,
Knight Books. At the outset Danny was told there would
be only two volumes in this game book series, but they
were so successful that several others followed. Danny's
method was to read through the book till the first really
good monster appeared and then set to work. Altogether,
he found them a very enjoyable set of commissions.
Danny does not play this kind of game, although he is
quite attracted to them. In his first week at Kingston art
college he and a fellow student spent a small fortune on
accessories for *Dungeons and Dragons*, little suspecting
the immense workload about to fall on their shoulders.
They still have not played their first game.

MUCH OF THE WORK DANNY PRODUCED before and during his foundation course was, he says: 'Weird Dali-esque stuff and Roger Dean impersonations, probably riddled with the stubbornness, naivety and arrogance of youth that is evident when you think you can run before you can walk.' Whatever the objective merit of these early pictures, they did point the direction in which he wanted to go.

But this did not happen immediately. As far as education was concerned Danny felt he'd had enough for the moment. When looking round at friends earning money, buying cars, taking girlfriends on holiday and generally experiencing life, he too wanted a piece of the action. So after Grimsby he did a variety of jobs including sign-writing, candle-making and working in a carpet store. The carpet shop was run by Poles, which resulted in him playing in a Polish football team on Sundays: 'The games were often hilarious affairs because half the team didn't wake up until midway through the second half, often nursing serious hangovers, yet somehow managed to turn in star performances. This was just as well really as we'd often be four or five goals down by then – if we were lucky.'

Then came a three-year stint driving overhead cranes at the local British Steel plant, which employed one sixth of the town's 60,000 population. For a while it was ideal because he was close to home and friends and had money for nightclubbing and holidays and all the other cash-consuming activities he wanted to explore. Work practices at the time (one reason, he suspects, why the plant no longer exists) meant that often there were three people doing one job, so for much of the time he was on standby, which gave him the opportunity to get down to some serious study of science fiction.

Among his favourite books at the time were *Neutron Star* by Larry Niven, almost everything by Michael Moorcock, but especially *Knight of Swords*, which still remains a favourite, the calendar of Moorcock illustrations *Wizardry,* and *Wild Romance* by Rodney Matthews and *Born with the Dead* by Robert Silverberg. Plus too many other titles to list, since he was getting through three or four books a week.

Danny's artistic talents, meanwhile, were not going to waste. His brush was in demand for decorating leather jackets, motorbikes and cars – including his own Austin 1100 which he covered with frogs and aliens. The car was stopped by the police so often that he sometimes wondered if they were perhaps checking to make sure it was being driven by an earthling.

Then on one particularly boring night shift he and an artistically inclined colleague decided to give their cabin a serious facelift: 'We proceeded to adorn the walls with aliens, wizards, spaceships, girls and snakes like some tattoo that had taken on a life of its own. Everyone loved it except for the shift manager who rewarded us with a few days suspension. The last I heard was that my partner in crime, Ray Leaning, eventually went on to be an Art Director at Marshall Cavendish.'

Throughout this period Danny continued to draw and paint the ideas that sprang from his reading, and he dreamt of drawing professionally. However, if anyone had predicted that within six years he would be doing exactly that, illustrating such grand masters of SF as Isaac Asimov, Arthur C. Clarke and Robert Heinlein, he would probably have laughed in disbelief. When the time came it felt surreal.

He was generally enjoying life in the steelworks, but as his twenty-first birthday approached he started to think more seriously about the future. Many of his friends were getting married and having kids and one side of Danny was drawn to this, but another recognized that if he was serious about becoming an illustrator family life would have to wait.

▶ **FIRE SWORD 1988**
GOUACHE AND INK.
11.02 x 16.1 IN. (28 x 41CM).
Cover for a book by Adrienne Martine-Barnes, Headline Press. The first of a set of four books in which the heroine falls asleep in modern Wiltshire and wakes up in medieval England. Or so it seems at first, but it turns out to be a very different place to the one she learnt about at school. In the background is Glastonbury Tor, where some of the action takes place. The border took Danny as long as the rest of the painting, which was unexpected and caused much cursing at the time, but Danny is pleased with the final result.

◀ RAINBOW SWORD 1989
GOUACHE AND INK.
11.02 x 16.1 IN. (28 x 41CM).
Cover for a book by Adrienne
Martine-Barnes, Headline Press.
Danny kept the stencils for the Celtic
borders of the first two books, but
this story was set in Greece, which
caused a slight design headache
and required a research trip to the
local library to study the
embellishments on Greek pottery.

▶ SEA SWORD 1990
GOUACHE AND INK.
11.02 x 16.1 IN. (28 x 41CM).
Cover for a book by Adrienne
Martine-Barnes, Headline Press.
Another change of border design was
required as the adventure moved to
the mystical East. As this was the
last book in the saga Danny let
himself go and really enjoyed
working on the painting.

While looking into the possibilities of furthering his education Danny began building up his portfolio, taking days off work to draw anything and everything that came to hand. A local museum proved a rich mine of subjects, as did the steelworks themselves, which with hindsight, Danny wishes he had concentrated on much more because of their imminent demise.

In choosing a college the main priority was to find one in the south near the publishing centres of London. On a tour of the possibilities he fell in love with Kingston Polytechnic where the staff were both friendly and helpful. Competition for places there was fierce at the time, with fifty or sixty contenders for each place, so having his application accepted was an immediate confidence booster. He was also very lucky with the timing because a few months before he

started the course the Normanby Park steelworks in Scunthorpe closed down. Whatever the reasons for the closure, it was a tragedy because the steelworks were the whole reason for the town's existence. For over a hundred years they had dominated the skyline and with their closure an estimated quarter of the working population was deprived of its income. A cloud of doom and gloom descended and Danny felt very lucky, almost guiltily so, at being able to escape. Armed with his redundancy money, he treated himself to holidays in France and the United States and then braced himself for a change.

The move in 1981 at the age of 23 from Scunthorpe in the north to Surrey, the archetypal southern county came as a distinct cultural shock for Danny, but he has never regretted it. Much as he loves the north and visits it regularly there is, he says: 'a certain gravity about northern towns that makes them hard to leave. Anything unusual in the way of lifestyle or career tends to be frowned on. If you want to be an artist or musician the most common advice is, "why not get a proper job instead?" Everyone wants you to do well, they really do, but they don't really believe you can.'

'The first term at college was the hardest three months I have ever known. I was shocked by the strictness and also the continuous threat of being thrown off the course if you did not keep up with the work. People imagine that art students have an easy life, but it wasn't like that at Kingston – at least, not to begin with. I remember being particularly panic-stricken at one stage as I was the only student who hadn't done any photography, beyond perhaps pressing the button of a "spit-out" Polaroid at the many eighteenth and twenty-first birthday parties around at that time.'

The five-year gap in his education had both positive and negative effects. The downside was that he was unused to painting or drawing every single day. He had grown accustomed to working when the mood took him and spending as long as he liked on a picture. At college unfinished assignments began to mount up around Danny. To organize himself he tried stacking the projects in different corners of his cramped hostel lodgings, but often it still felt like a losing battle.

However, on the plus side he feels that being a 'mature student' with a taste of the real working world probably gave him a clearer sense of purpose than he would otherwise have had, a greater willingness to work and the resilience to cope with the frustrations he met. The value of this seemed to be recognized by the college because out of that year's intake of forty students about five others had also been out in the 'real world' for a while.

Being surrounded by like-minded souls was great for Danny, but also rather daunting. At school he had grown used to being the best artist around, but now he found himself amongst stiff competition. It was simultaneously uplifting and he says, 'rather humbling'. What he also felt strongly, even at the start of the course, was the probability that some of his fellow students were likely to become friends for life, which has in fact happened.

The course was a BA Honours degree in Graphic Design, which to begin with was devoted to perfecting basic skills such as typography and studio methods. At the end of the first year came a choice between graphic design and illustration; the class was split evenly between the two. Since it had always been his ambition, Danny chose illustration which, he believes, is the tougher option. Certainly it is the more insecure one because illustrators are basically on their own, whereas designers tend to work in teams and good ones often end up with lucrative jobs in advertising: 'Many of the adverts I now see on TV are done by ex-colleagues of mine. I always look at the end of any program credits to see if the graphic designer was at Kingston – often they were.'

▶LORD OF THE EAGLES **1992**
GOUACHE AND INK.
10.2 x 14.1 IN. (26 x 36CM).
Private work. Tolkien has, fairly naturally, long been one of Danny's favourite authors. One of the treats of living near Oxford is occasionally visiting the Eagle and Child pub where Tolkien, C.S. Lewis and other members of their informal literary group, the Inklings, used to meet for often heated debates about mythology, art and the meaning of life generally. If commissioned, Danny would happily spend the rest of his life illustrating the works of Tolkien and Mervyn Peake, whose books he regularly re-reads. With this picture he has made a start, basing it on one of Tolkien's own illustrations for *The Hobbit*.

▲ SUCCUBUS 1993
GOUACHE AND INK. 10.6 x 14.5 IN. (27 x 37CM).
Private work. Where this idea came from Danny has no clue. It
was one of those images that appeared to take shape of its own
accord and nag at him till it was painted. A similar thing often
happens with certain colour combinations, in this case purple and
blue. The lacy atmospheric effect was achieved by airbrushing
through a real piece of lace, a process that is rather
unpredictable, but which he has used effectively elsewhere. The
contrast between the strange and the ordinary is a favourite
device. In this case the slightly disturbing female and the ordinary
thistle and bee give the desired effect. Danny could have
continued adding details to this picture indefinitely, but instinct
warned him that doing so would dilute the image.

▶ CHASM OF DOOM 1993
GOUACHE AND INK. 10.6 x 14.9 IN. (27 x 38CM).
This is based on a cover Danny painted for a
volume in the *Lone Wolf Fighting Fantasy Saga*.
The original sadly 'disappeared' while in the
hands of the publishers. This is an
occupational hazard for illustrators and when it
first happened Danny was quite upset, but
over the years he has in fact escaped lightly
and is almost able to accept such losses as
roundabout compliments. Often, as in this
case, it means he can do the picture again
properly without the pressure of meeting a
fierce deadline.

◀ **SILENT TOWER 1993**
GOUACHE AND INK. 12.5 x 19.6 IN. (32 x 50CM).
Private work. This piece began life in 1986 as a cover
illustration for a story of the same name by Barbara
Hambly. Although it got as far as the proof stage it
was not actually used in the end, so Danny reworked
it extensively some time later.

▼ **INVADERS FROM THE CENTRE 1987**
GOUACHE AND INK. 8.6 x 12.9 IN. (22 x 33CM).
Cover for a book by Brian Stableford, Hodder and Stoughton.
This was the second volume in a trilogy that Danny enjoyed
for the strange assortment of creatures and alien cultures.
The cover had an unusual diamond-shaped area for the
illustration, which meant leaving the corners blank.

◀ **BLOODSWORD II: THE KINGDOM OF WYRD 1986**
GOUACHE AND INK. 7.8 x 12.5 IN. (20 x 32CM).
Cover for a book by Dave Morris and Oliver Johnson,
Knight Books. The first two volumes of this series
were released simultaneously and carried a
promotional competition for limited-edition prints of
the covers. To enter readers were required to answer
questions relating to the text. Presenting the prizes
involved a day's visit to the company's head office.
Danny was very flattered by his reception, but was
then brought swiftly down to earth by finding some of
his own covers in the line of unsold books on their
way to the pulping machine.

▲ **BLOODSWORD III: THE DEMON'S CLAW 1987**
GOUACHE AND INK. 7.8 x 12.5 IN. (20 x 32CM).
Cover for a book by Dave Morris and Oliver Johnson, Knight
Books. The satisfying thing about this picture was that it
gave Danny the opportunity to use an idea that came to
him years before while he worked at British Steel.
Sometimes, when bored on the night shift, he collected
scraps of waste molten iron (after they had cooled, of
course) and improvised them into alien creatures in his
sketchpad. One of these preliminary sketches provided the
model for this monster. According to Danny, the moral of
the story is, never throw anything away because you never
know when it might come in useful.

CHAPTER THREE

THE DARK SIDE

TANK OF SERPENTS 1986
GOUACHE AND INK.
8.6 x 11.8 IN. (22 x 30CM).
Cover for a book by James Leasor, Collins. When he
began this picture Danny saw few problems ahead but
ended up having to model the snakes in Plasticine
and poise his desk lamp over them to get the
shadows and highlights. Having delivered the artwork
for this cover Danny called into a small café and
found himself sitting next to his greatest football
hero, the legendary George Best.

MOST OF THE TUTORS AT KINGSTON POLYTECHNIC were active professionals who taught part time. On arrival, the name Harry Willock on the roster caught Danny's eye. 'I know that name,' he thought, 'but surely it can't be the same man.' The person he was thinking of was Alan Aldridge's collaborator on *The Butterfly Ball, Peacock Party* and a number of other lavishly illustrated children's books, and also on record covers, for example, Elton John's *Captain Fantastic.* Willock was the technician on these projects, and he worked up Aldridge's ideas and sketches into lovingly detailed and richly coloured illustrations rather like a steel engraver did in the past.

It was the same man, and as a tutor Willock was as entertaining as he was helpful. He had a remarkably youthful manner, loved his work and appeared to have had none of his humour beaten out of him by life. He became another of Danny's guiding lights and they still keep in touch.

The college frequently invited successful artists in for one-off visits, which were tremendously inspiring for Danny, because they showed that for all its insecurities illustration could work as a career. Chief among these artists in Danny's recollection is Michael Foreman, one of the most successful children's book illustrators in the country.

In the second year the pressure of work eased and there was less of a feeling that you might be thrown out on your ear at any moment. As projects the students were given records, books and magazine articles to illustrate, which was all very well, but often Danny felt frustrated at not being able to do what he had gone there to learn, which was fantasy illustration. At times, he felt so bombarded with different styles and trends that he found it hard to remember or develop his own approach. Most of the time, however, he gritted his teeth and went along with it, experimenting with all that was suggested – large and small format pictures, sketchy or detailed technique. But on occasions he felt as if he were being brainwashed. However, looking back on this period he is more sanguine: 'College is, after all, the ideal environment in which to experiment and try different things, and there is always the possibility of discovering a new technique.'

At around this time a local advertising studio ran a competition, they wanted a black and white illustration on the subject of the Titanic disaster. Tempted by the prospect of a £100 first prize Danny entered. 'My piece was a rather scribbly attempt,' he remembers, 'which, in fact, I'd ripped off and doctored from an old etching done at the time of the sinking. The end result looked dreadful to me and I remember gingerly adding my "masterpiece" to the bottom of the pile of entrants. I thought no more of it, until to everyone's amazement, especially my own, I won. As well as the prize money I was treated to a lavish meal at a local restaurant. You just never know what people are going to like.'

High points for Danny in the second year were the straight drawing exercises, either on outdoor location or in the studio. These sessions were very effective in sharpening an art student's power of observation, and the strict time limits that were sometimes enforced meant having to draw and paint more by instinct than calculation. Danny came to appreciate these skills more when it came to producing ideas for book jackets more or less instantly. He also found the 'crits' sessions valuable, during these students were required to present their latest project to a group of peers for evaluation and assessment. This was often a traumatic experience but ultimately useful in gaining a degree of objectivity towards your own work. But overall the year left him feeling somewhat dissatisfied.

He had managed to introduce traces of fantasy into his college work but felt he had yet to show what he was really capable of doing.

▶ **FAMILY PORTRAIT 1986**
GOUACHE AND INK.
9.4 x 14.1 IN. (24 x 36CM).
Cover for a book by Graham Masterton, Arrow Books. This was Danny's first horror illustration. The book had a big promotional budget with posters of the cover scattered all over London – on hoardings and on the sides of buses. Danny found this pleasantly disconcerting, but also very welcome as he needed all the encouragement he could get at the time. The story is loosely based on that of Dorian Gray, to whom the main character is related, and tells of a family trying to get hold of the painting in the title.

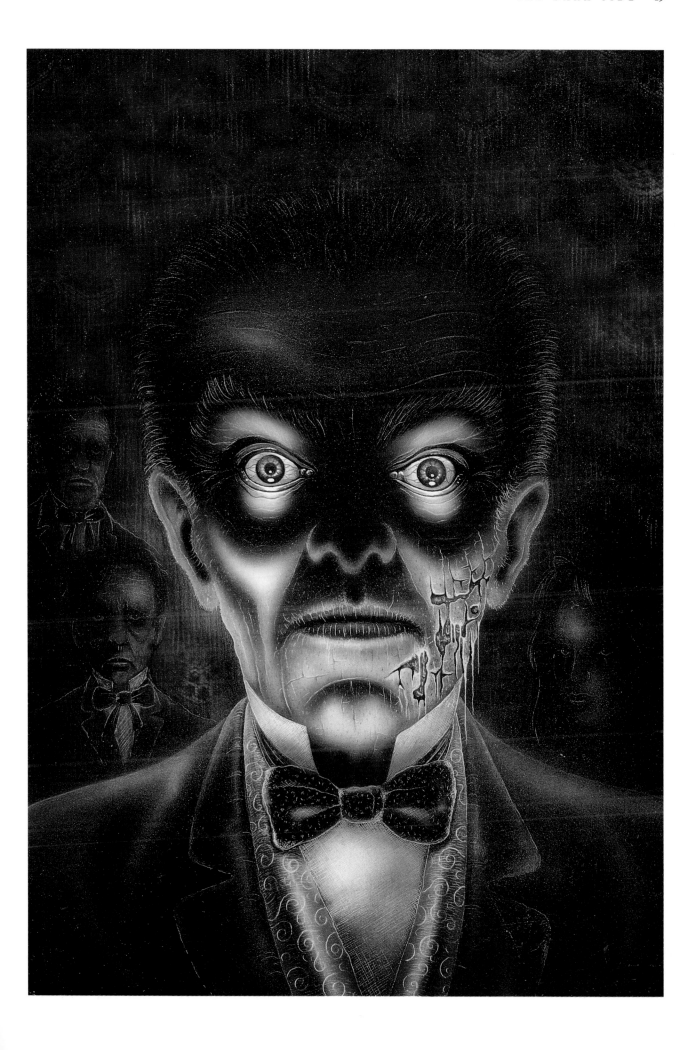

To add to his discomfort he received poor grades despite having worked very hard. This added insult to injury; having being forced to concentrate on subjects in which he had no great interest it seemd unjust to be penalized for showing a lack of flair. Looking back on it he now wonders if this was deliberate college policy designed to enable students to focus fully on their strengths by providing opportunities for displaying their weaknesses.

However, at the time all he could see was the apparent injustice of it all, and that summer, while on the island of Thassos in Greece, he did some serious thinking and decided the time had come to show what he could do on his own terms. Also, he was very conscious of having only a year left before facing the real world again and this gave an edge to his determination. An immediate step was to begin a series of watercolours of the Greek islands, which he is fascinated by and continues to explore year by year, loving not only the beautiful scenery and lighting but also the mythology in which they are steeped.

While on Thassos he also began planning his final year's thesis, a major part of the course in which students were given a fairly free rein. What came to mind was the outline of a kind of mini-novel in which aliens come to earth to find the reasons for the current surge of interest in science fiction films. Disguised as a reporter, one of the aliens accosts Danny himself on his way to see *Return of the Jedi* and in the course of questioning elicits from him a brief history of SF films up to the *Star Wars* series, which changed the way such films have been made ever since. In the story Danny remains unsuspecting of the true nature of his interlocutor till near the end, and even then there remains an element of uncertainty.

This suggestion went down well with Danny's tutors and he kicked off the final year on a promising note. Other freedoms followed and Danny found himself being positively encouraged to build up his portfolio with examples of the kind of work he hoped to do professionally. What he felt was needed was fifteen to twenty high-quality fantasy paintings. For general work he chose his favourite novels (rather neglected since the beginning of the course) and designed new covers for them, while his major project was loosely based on *The Dancers at the End of Time* trilogy by Michael Moorcock. For this he produced five paintings in a montage style more akin to film posters than book covers. These he rates as his first serious attempt to do the kind of work he does now although, with hindsight, he says: 'I was almost trying too hard with most of them, cramming too much into them. I have since learned, and am still learning, that often it's what is left out of a picture that makes it good. I still feel as if I'm serving a long apprenticeship.'

An example of his college work is METAMORPHOSIS on page 17. Despite having provided covers for many of the other big names in fantasy Danny has yet to be asked to paint one for Moorcock, which is a lingering regret.

The degree show on 8 June 1984 imposed fierce pressures and was an enormous last-minute test of confidence. Rather than hover anxiously by his own display Danny wandered about or nipped off to the pub with several of the other stressed students, returning occasionally to eavesdrop on viewer's comments – which were generally encouraging. Even more encouraging, 'brilliant for confidence' in fact, were the number of business cards left by art directors and the like who visit such shows looking for fresh talent. Also, the kind and complimentary words that total strangers had written in the Comments Book left on the stand.

Then followed a great sense of anticlimax, slight humiliation even as, armed with his degree, Danny signed on the dole and felt he was

▶ **THE CENTRE CANNOT HOLD 1989**
GOUACHE AND INK.
90.4 x 15.7 IN. (24 x 40CM).
Cover for a book by Brian Stableford, New English Library. A problem Danny encountered with this picture was concentrating on such an eerie image while the outside world was flooded with glorious June sunshine. In addition, Danny's then girlfriend had just walked out on him. He discovered at the time that emotional turmoil is no help at all with horror illustration, the best frame of mind is a totally peaceful one.

back at the bottom of the heap. After the frenzy of the previous few months there was a strong temptation to do nothing except relax and unwind for a while, but this was countered by the need to do something to get his career off the ground.

Luckily he was not alone. He and three college friends in the same predicament rented a house in the London suburb of Surbiton and together set about following up the business leads they had and trying to think of others. June to December was taken up with almost daily, but mostly fruitless visits, to publishing houses in the city and arranging meetings that rarely came to anything. Meeting art directors who were used to dealing with the country's best artists was a daunting experience. Most were helpful, and offered constructive advice even if they had no work to offer, but one in particular (who, after some wrestling with conscience, shall remain nameless) stands out in Danny's memory as being particularly cruel and hurtful, verbally tearing his work apart and saying that Danny would never get anywhere. Fortunately, some of Danny's friends had received similar treatment so the impact was diminished. It helped a lot that he was sharing a house with others in the same predicament. Unless one counts the occasion when, in the middle of a promising interview, Danny opened his portfolio to find that in the rush to catch the morning train he had picked up someone else's by mistake.

Most of these efforts appeared to be a waste except in terms of learning a little more about life, but odd bits of employment did crop up. The first of any note was a commission for the covers of some relaxation music. The company, New World Cassettes, is now one of the largest publishers of relaxation tapes in Europe, but it was then in its infancy and it was exciting to be in on the venture from the beginning. Danny was given a fairly free hand, being presented with the music and a title, for example, *Secret Garden*, *Spirit of the Red Man* or *Ascension*, and then left pretty much to his own devices. The artwork was enjoyed by the musicians and it was great for Danny to see his work in print at last. Many of the tapes are still available with his designs.

Then, having by this time made the round of all the publishers he could think of, Danny began the circuit again, his credibility having gone up a notch through having some published work to show. Shaking off the 'student' tag was a big hurdle for Danny. He comments: 'No matter how good it is, unpublished work seems to count for less than almost anything in print.'

His next real break came from Puffin Books with a commission for the covers of three children's books featuring the character Pippi Longstocking. Why he was chosen is still a slight mystery because he hadn't done work like it before. Unless it was because Danny wore odd socks at the interview like the main character, a habit he still has. If he happens to pull two matching socks out of the drawer in the morning he puts one back and tries again.

Danny thought it was great to be involved with a series of books that are well known around the world and have been made into successful children's films. In early 1985, perhaps as a result of this commission, things began to move.

From Steve Lang, the art director at Arrow Books, came Danny's first chance to illustrate some adult books, crime-detective novels including *Death of Unicorn* and *Lizard in a Cup* by Peter Dickinson; plus some aliens for a couple of covers for the *Lone Wolf Fighting Fantasy* saga. The first of these required an octopus-like creature and because it was a chance to show what he could do in this field Danny wanted to pull out all the stops, but he had only a weekend to complete the picture so the result was a slight disappointment. He later repainted it to get it right.

▶ **AND DISREGARDS THE REST** 1992
GOUACHE AND INK.
12.6 x 18.1 IN. (32 x 46CM).
Cover for a book by Paul Voermans, Victor Gollancz. Danny asked a crazy friend of his if he would mind having his photograph taken on the lawn being struck by lightning. 'He kindly obliged,' said Danny, 'and came round in the works van of his plumbing business, which always turns a few heads because welded to the outside is a full-size white bath complete with taps, plug and drain.'

Around this time Danny was also given his first crack at horror illustration, being presented with the first few chapters of an eagerly awaited novel by Graham Masterton. With Steve Lang's help, Danny came up with the idea of an enticing double cover in which the main characters of the story stare menacingly out of an overlaid, gold-embossed window in which a broken pane of glass neatly obscures half a rotten face waiting to assault the eye when the outer cover is lifted.

▼ BOUNDARIES 1991
GOUACHE AND INK. 4.7 x 10.2 IN. (12 x 26CM).
Cover for a book by T.M. Wright, Victor Gollancz. While reading this story about an agoraphobic Danny noticed an attractive girl in his local pub who he thought would be ideal for the cover. The problem in such situations, though, is that however delicately you choose your words they end up sounding very much like: 'Would you like to come up and see my etchings?' Fortunately, in this instance it turned out that they had a mutual acquaintance and when asked to pose the girl was quite willing.

As a horror debut, FAMILY PORTRAIT (p.48) was a great success and opened the way to much more work in the same line. He sees his facility with the subject as just a kind of happy accident proceeding from the skills he acquired in other branches of fantasy. The irony of this is that Danny is not a particular fan of horror and is also fairly squeamish, having recently visited the dentist for only the fourth time in his life.

Danny finds that many people who meet him after seeing his horror work have very odd expectations; they imagine him to be some kind of tortured soul plagued by nightmares – but he very rarely has these and then only when under severe pressure. Many others also have a strange reaction, looking at him afresh with an expression that resembles something from the pictures.

As an example of how there need be no contradiction between doing and enjoying this kind of work, Danny cites the case of Peter Cushing who has acted in countless creepy horror films while remaining in everyday life a perfectly charming and sane English gentleman. In fact, simply an actor doing his job, just as illustrators do theirs.

Overleaf
TEMPTER 1991
GOUACHE AND INK.
5.9 x 9.8 IN. (15 x 25CM).
Cover for a book. Danny had to do this illustration in a hurry for this steamy vampire story. He remembers being surprised to see the finished book so soon after completion, while in the departure lounge at Gatwick Airport, as he set off for a lazy week in Greece.

◀ **WEREWOLVES OF LONDON 1989**
GOUACHE AND INK.
11.8 x 17.7 IN. (30 x 45CM).
Cover for a book by Brian
Stableford, Simon and Schuster.
Danny was looking for a timeless
and ghostly look to give this girl, but
found he could not achieve it till he
deliberately spaced her eyes slightly
wider apart than usual.

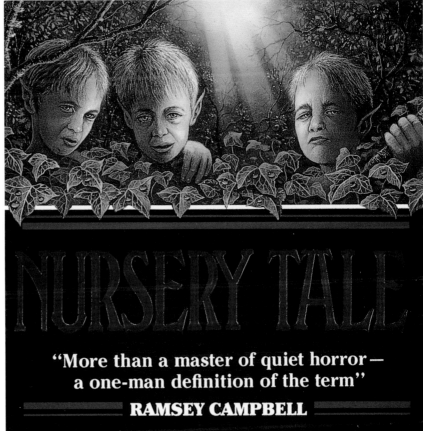

▼▶ **NURSERY TALE 1993**
GOUACHE AND INK.
3.5 x 8.2 IN. (9 x 21CM).
Cover for a book by T.M. Wright,
Victor Gollancz. A local delicatessen
did well out of Danny on the day he
took reference photographs for this
picture. A friend's little boy, Henry,
and two of his schoolmates needed
a constant supply of fancy cakes and
orange juice to entice them to pull
the faces required.

▼ **THE SCHOOL 1992**
GOUACHE AND INK. 3.9 x 8.4 IN. (10 x 21.5CM).
Cover for a book by T.M. Wright, Victor Gollancz. Danny was working late at
night on this picture and was deep in concentration with Brian Eno's *The Pearl*
playing softly in the background when thwack a careless owl smashed into the
window. 'It nearly gave me a heart attack,' said Danny 'and caused me to
scatter paints, brushes and inks everywhere, including over half the painting.'

▼ **STRANGE SEED 1992**
GOUACHE AND INK. 4.3 x 9.05 IN. (11 x 23CM).
Unpublished version. There are two versions of this
picture because Danny was asked to modify his first
submission for publication. It is quite common as an
illustrator to imagine that you are on the same
wavelength as the art director who commissioned
the piece, but in fact, when the work is submitted
you find this is not the case. Whether the change
was an improvement is for the reader to judge.

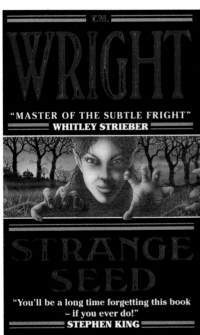

◄ **STRANGE SEED 1992**
GOUACHE AND INK.
4.3 x 9.0 IN. (11 x 23CM).
Cover for a book by T.M. Wright,
Victor Gollancz. 'After a long day
spent putting the finishing touches
on to this painting I needed a
break so I called into a nearby pub
for a couple of quiet beers. On
leaving I mentioned to the landlord
that I had an hour's work left to do
on the painting and he asked if he
could call round to see the
finished article. Presuming he
meant the next morning I said yes.
So, imagine my surprise when half
an hour later, not only the
landlord, but most of the pub's
clientele – all in various stages of
inebriation – came marching into
my studio.'

◀ **LITTLE BOY LOST 1990**
GOUACHE AND INK.
4.3 x 9.4 IN. (11 x 24CM).
Cover for a book by T.M. Wright,
Victor Gollancz. In typical Wright
style, the author creates a
frightening scenario from the most
mundane of situations. In this book
a father and his two sons nip down
to the local supermarket, and as the
father parks his car, one of his sons
literally vanishes before his eyes.

▼ **THE PLACE 1990**
GOUACHE AND INK. 4.3 x 9.4 IN. (11 x 24CM).
Cover for a book by T.M. Wright, Victor Gollancz. This commission
provided a good excuse for Danny to use cats. He adores the creatures
and loves painting them, but unfortunately, he is allergic to them.

▲ MANHATTAN GHOST STORY **1989**
GOUACHE AND INK. 8.6 x 13.7 IN. (22 x 35CM).
Cover for a book by T.M. Wright, Victor Gollancz. This story is currently
being made into a major film, possibly starring Sharon Stone.

▶▲ WILD SEED 1991

GOUACHE AND INK.

4.3 x 9.4 IN. (11 x 24CM)

Cover for a book by Octavia Butler, Victor Gollancz. Seeing the jacket proofs for the first time, according to Danny, is always the cause of some trepidation, since one has no idea what the typographer has in mind. On this occasion, a young trainee did the lettering as his first assignment and Danny thinks he did an excellent job.

▼ **THE LAST VAMPIRE 1990**
GOUACHE AND INK. 4.7 x 9.8 IN. (12 x 25CM).
Cover for a book by T.M. Wright, Victor
Gollancz. A source of secret delight to Danny
is that few people immediately notice that in
this picture there are two rats snarling at
each other, not a single one menacing the
viewer. The motif surfaces in a few other
paintings.

▲ **PROTEUS UNBOUND 1988**
GOUACHE AND INK.
8.6 x 13.7 IN. (22 x 35CM).
Cover for a book by Charles
Sheffield, Hodder and Stoughton.

◄ **SIGHT OF PROTEUS 1987**
GOUACHE AND INK.
8.6 x 13.7 IN. (22 x 35CM).
Cover for a book by Charles
Sheffield, Hodder and Stoughton.
Whenever possible, Danny likes to
read a book thoroughly before
tackling the illustration, and this is
something he likes to do in bed. He
remembers opening this one,
propped up against the pillows, and
not being able to close it again till he
heard the milkman's bottles clinking
outside and realized dawn was
breaking. 'It was very strange
hearing the distant noise of cars and
realizing everyone else was
beginning their tomorrow, while I
hadn't yet finished yesterday.' This
novel portrays a future where it is
fashionable to have one's body
changed into almost anything one
desires. Such is the advanced state
of medical science that all this is
possible, but weird things begin to
happen as ordinary humans turn into
bizarre, glowing-eyed aliens.
According to Danny it is 'a kind of
sci-fi Inspector Morse mystery.'

▲ THE DRIVE IN 1989
GOUACHE AND INK.
10.2 x 15.7 IN. (26 x 40CM).
Cover for a book by Joe Lansdale,
Hodder and Stoughton. Painting this
cover proved to be more of a
nightmare for Danny than the story
itself. Everything possible went
wrong with the job and the final
jacket was a combination of about
three different illustrations skilfully
stitched together by the printers.

◀ RELICS 1986
GOUACHE AND INK.
9.05 x 12.9 IN. (23 x 33CM).
Cover for a book by Shaun Hutson, W.H.
Allen. Danny: 'I have never met Shaun
Hutson but I understand that he only started
writing himself after reading a seriously over-
the-top novel about a plague of crabs.
Almost for fun he wrote a story about killer
slugs in a similar vein and it went on to
become a best-seller. Interestingly, those
people who are most critical of horror stories
have often never read one and consquently
don't realize that many of the stories are
written tongue in cheek, and even those that
aren't usually end on an optimistic note.'

▲ SHADOWS 1986
GOUACHE AND INK.
9.05 x 12.9 IN. (23 x 33CM).
Cover for a book by Shaun
Hutson, W.H. Allen. With
this picture Danny was
trying to illustrate the
popular notion that we
each carry an angel and a
demon within us. In
general, he tries to avoid
particularly gruesome
images, but being thankful
that he does not work in a
hospital, he does not mind
occasionally.

◀ SHATTER 1990
GOUACHE AND INK.
9.4 x 14.1 IN. (24 x 36CM).
Cover for a book by John Farris,
Victor Gollancz. According to Danny
very little is needed to make dolls
look strange because they are pretty
strange things anyway. The only
change he made to the Victorian doll
was to damage the eye.

▼ HONEYSUCKLE SPIDER WEB 1989
GOUACHE AND INK.
12.9 x 18.8 IN. (33 x 48CM).
Cover for *The Wexford Omnibus* by
Ruth Rendell, Arrow Books. Danny
still has difficulty believing when, for
example, watching a Ruth Rendell
play on television that the shops are
full of books by her with his artwork
on the cover. It still doesn't seem
that long ago since he was driving
overhead cranes for British Steel.

▲ PSYCLONE 1989
GOUACHE AND INK.
8.6 x 13.7 IN. (22 x 35CM).
Cover for a book by Greg Bear, Victor
Gollancz. Thinking he'd done a
painting that would please the art
director, especially as the rough
preliminary sketch had been warmly
received, Danny was most
disgruntled at having to paint out the
house and move it a bit nearer the
spout. 'It did improve the picture as
it happened but,' admits Danny, 'it
was not easy to appreciate this at
the time.'

▲ BAD BLOOD 1990
GOUACHE AND INK.
9.4 x 14.1 IN. (24 x 36CM).
Cover for a book by John Farris,
Victor Gollancz. Often with horror
pictures Danny likes to introduce
a contrast by, for example,
having an idyllic sunset in the
background of an otherwise
sinister composition. In this
case, he tried as hard as
possible to make the church
appear as a safe haven; he
spent as long painting the church
as he did the creature.

▼ FEVRE DREAM 1987
GOUACHE AND INK.
4.7 x 10.2 IN. (12 x 26CM).
Cover for a book by George R. Martin, Victor Gollancz.
Before he even began thinking of ideas for this cover
Danny read the book twice, and rates it among his top
ten favourite novels of all time. The book title is the
name of a steamboat on the Mississippi. The story
gives a sympathetic account of vampires, which made
Danny feel rather sorry for them by the end. When first
published the book failed to cause any great stir, but
the publishers felt it was worth reissuing with a fresh
cover and commissioned Danny. He came up with the
idea of having a narrow strip of illustration across a
black background. Whether coincidentally or not, the
book was a great success this time and the cover
format was extended by Gollancz to many other titles,
and now many other leading horror publishers also
use it.

The image was suggested to Danny by a beautiful
descriptive passage where the captain realizes, while
watching the sun set over the river, that something
strange is going on – the realization grows stronger
and stronger as the sky changes from orange to
crimson to deep blood red...

▲ **METAL MESSIAH 1989**
Gouache and Ink,
15.7 x 15.7 in. (40 x 40cm)
Record cover, Hardcore
Management. While still living in
Scunthorpe, Danny and a friend once
jokingly discussed going into
partnership in the music business –
one producing records, the other
decorating sleeves. Years later the
joke materialized when the same
friend commissioned this cover for a
heavy metal/thrash band.

▲ **TREAD SOFTLY 1986**
GOUACHE AND INK.
8.6 x 13.7 IN. (22 x 35CM).
Cover for a book by Richard Kelly, W.H. Allen. Danny
painted this picture shortly after moving to Oxford and
planned to combine its delivery with a pleasant weekend
visiting friends in London. After putting the finishing
touches to it on the Friday he started tidying his things
away. Unfortunately, he picked up a bottle of white ink
the top of which was not properly fastened and in a flash
it became a white volcano that planted itself in the
middle of the painting, completely obliterating a week's
work. Danny screamed so loud he lost his voice for
several days and instead of his planned trip to London
the weekend was spent furiously rescuing the picture.

▶ **FLESH 1987**
GOUACHE AND INK.
9.05 x 13.7 IN. (23 x 35CM).
Cover for a book by Richard Laymon,
W.H. Allen. A particularly unpleasant
though well-written tale about slug-
like parasites that eat the body away
from within. Danny's first cover,
which was used on the hardback,
was considered almost too
disturbing so he was asked to
rework it and tone it down for the
paperback version.

CHAPTER FOUR

SPACE MACHINES

ZARATHUSTRA 1990
GOUACHE AND INK.
11.8 x 20.07 IN. (30 x 51CM).
Computer game cover, Hewson Games. To get the feel
of this game Danny was lent a copy; he became so
addicted to it that he almost ran out of time to finish the
picture. A friend of his used to call round every evening
to see how the picture was progressing and then, as a
further distraction, frequently persuaded Danny to go out
for a drink. When the artwork came back from the
publishers Danny gave it to him as a memento.

IN HIS TOUR OF PUBLISHERS after graduating from Kingston Danny found Ian Hughes, the Art Director at Hodder and Stoughton, especially helpful and constructive in both his praise and criticism. No work was immediately forthcoming, but on each visit Danny ensured he had at least a couple of new paintings to show – believing, or perhaps merely hoping, that sooner or later he would be given a book to illustrate. So it turned out: 'and what a book it was to begin with, namely *The Cat Who Walks Through Walls*, the newest novel by the SF author Robert A. Heinlein. This was an important and exciting breakthrough for me and to this day I still feel extremely grateful to Ian Hughes for this and all the other projects he gave me in 1986.'

Other top authors he was given to illustrate included Frederik Pohl, Isaac Asimov and Arthur C. Clarke, which gave a tremendous boost to Danny's professional profile. Despite all the sweat and patience it took to reach this, his original goal, on arrival he felt almost surprised it had not taken longer. Six years seemed quite a brief time to metamorphose from a football-playing steelworker with artistic ambitions into a fully fledged illustrator of top-flight authors in his favourite genre.

There were aspects of this breakthrough that were rather alarming though, for example, knowing that sooner or later he was going to be asked to paint a spaceship. In this area he felt totally overshadowed by earlier illustrators who had carried it off so triumphantly – from Chris Foss, who more or less established a monopoly in spaceship design in the late 70s and early 80s, through Tim White, Peter Jones and Jim Burns. He also felt handicapped by having no great interest in technology itself. With cars in everyday life, for example, he only really pays attention to their colour and style and has not the faintest curiosity about what goes on under the bonnet. In SF it is the possibilities opened up by space travel that interest him more than the machinery that could make it possible.

So, he awaited the first request for a spaceship with much trepidation. It eventually came with the cover for *Oceans of Venus* by Isaac Asimov. Swallowing his doubts, Danny forced himself just to get stuck into it and try to come up with something that looked fast and as if it might work. A little to his surprise, the art director liked it and the rest of the series followed, all requiring spaceships.

Suddenly finding his work in demand, Danny found he had to tread a fine line at first between being original and meeting the expectations of his clients, that is operating within parameters defined by preceding and currently successful illustrators. Some general similarities were unavoidable, but as far as possible he didn't want his work to look like anyone else's and avoided any conscious plagiarism. The fear of unconsciously lifting other people's ideas, though, was worrying to begin with: 'At the ideas stage of a commission you hope that whatever you have thought up is an original concept, but you can sit forever weighing up all the ifs and buts, do's and don'ts. At some point you simply have to knuckle down and get on with the job.'

'As more work comes in and your confidence grows you become more "yourself". This is particularly true after the thrill of seeing your work on a bookshop shelf, a novelty that never really wears off. Through a process of trial, and more especially error, a personal style develops.'

What also develops is a general work method: 'A typical painting, obviously, starts off as a vast expanse of white. In all honesty, I don't enjoy mapping out a painting but it is one of those necessary evils. Usually, I can hardly wait to get the colours out but that extra bit of time and patience can often be vital. The hardest work is done

▶ **BIG SUN OF MERCURY 1987**
GOUACHE AND INK.
8.3 x 12.9 IN. (21.2 x 33CM).
Cover for a book by Isaac Asimov, Lightning Books. One of a series of six books, which were originally commissioned to another artist. However, having completed the first one he mysteriously disappeared, and the work was passed to Danny. This image was prompted by memories of the Flixborough disaster on 1 June, 1974 when the Nypro chemical factory just outside Scunthorpe blew up, shattering almost every window within twenty miles (thirty-two kilometres).

at the ideas stage, furiously trying to think up an image or scene that is both eyecatching and representative of what the book is about. And yes, I do occasionally get the "creative block" where nothing suitable comes.

'In the first stage my scribbles tend to be a mess, very loose and even abstract as I toy with shapes, weights, composition, light source and so on until I begin to see in my mind something that will work.' Danny usually works with a 2B pencil or black felt pen on a layout pad, which has tissue-like paper transparent enough for line drawings to show through from one layer to the next. Embryonic ideas can thus be developed gradually by adding or taking away a bit here and there as one leaf overlaps another, and another, until something substantial appears. He may then experiment with colours, adding a hint of possible choices, although nothing too specific at this stage.

'Usually I only send one, or perhaps two, strong ideas into the publishers for approval. For the artwork itself I usually use CS10 illustration board which is as smooth as porcelain. In fact, it contains a percentage of kaolin that helps absorb airbrush ink enabling many layers of colour to be superimposed, producing wonderful depths in skies. Unfortunately, such depth is often lost to a degree in printing.'

Normally, Danny begins by airbrushing the skies then gradually works to the foreground where the main image is painted with fine sable brushes. Sometimes for doing fur or distant grassblades he uses a scalpel, which cuts through to the white of the board. Whilst working on a painting he surrounds the drawing board with relevant reference pictures. As with most illustrators, he keeps a large stock of such photographic material, often culled from colour supplements and bargains from cheap bookshops which are filed in scrapbooks under headings such as trees, snowy landscapes, ideas for alien cities, weird jewellery and so on.

'Paintings usually take between forty to eighty hours depending on their complexity. As you can imagine, it is not exactly physically straining to be sat at a drawing board all day. There is the danger of eyestrain perhaps, but a long country walk staring at distant hills and trees is a good antidote. Sometimes a walk is essential anyway, especially if a painting is going slowly or doesn't look right. Holding a paintbrush for hours at a time can stiffen up the fingers but for this nothing works better than a spell at my electronic keyboards. I would like to explore creative music much more in the future and practise when I can, but I don't think Vangelis need worry yet. The attraction of music is that the mood and result is instant whereas painting requires much more patience and time in the build-up. But the fun of painting is trying to get there, being a god of sorts when creating a believable environment or creature from nothing except rough sketches, reference photos, paints and brushes.

'It's a great feeling when the last two hours or so come along and you're putting the final touches to a painting – the highlight on an eye, the shadow on a tower – and the components all gel to the point when some mysterious instinct says to stop.'

Despite his experience, Danny is still a little daunted when the moment comes to lift the cover paper and reveal his masterpiece to an art director. 'The five-second silence that follows seems to last hours. One prays that one has delivered a better illustration than suggested by the approved visual rough, and there is no better feeling when this happens, but it is hard not to take it personally when you have to take the picture home for minor alterations.'

Having achieved lift-off as an illustrator Danny felt secure enough not to have to live any longer on the fringe of London. In June 1986 he moved to Oxfordshire to be with his long-term girlfriend, and since then his work has been in steady demand in several different

▶ **PIRATES OF ASTEROIDS 1987**
GOUACHE AND INK.
8.3 x 12.9 IN. (21.2 x 33CM).
Cover for a book by Isaac Asimov, Lightning Books. This was the second in the Space Ranger series featuring the adventures of the character David Starr. The image was suggested to Danny by an incredible scene in the film, *The Empire Strikes Back*, where the Millenium Falcon is chased through an asteroid field by three of Darth Vader's TIE fighters.

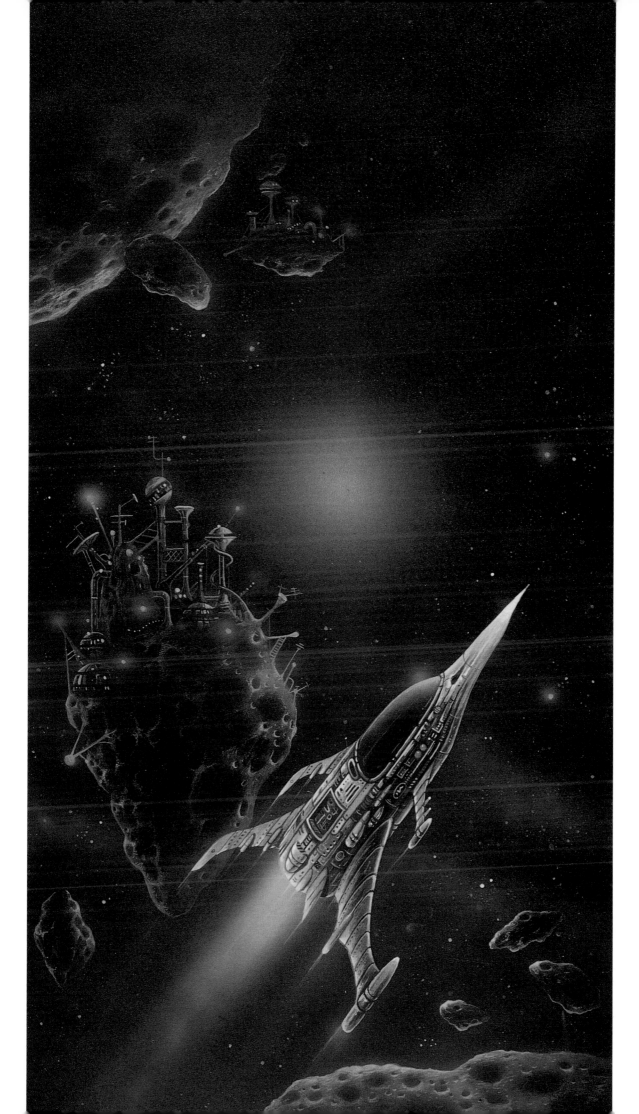

fields of illustration. As steady, that is, as demand ever is in the notoriously volatile life of an illustrator. With the ups and downs of publishing and the general economic climate Danny tends to be either swamped with work or left twiddling his thumbs wondering how to pay the next month's bills. 'If you have to turn down work because you are so busy, people tend not to ring back again when you need it. Also, success can be counterproductive because certain art directors assume your fees have risen beyond their budget.'

Even when things are going well, Danny finds that staying in business demands a never-ending process of marketing his work because art directors and companies are constantly changing. He was once told: 'The people who work for us are generally people we see.' And Danny comments, 'You have to show your face otherwise when work comes along no-one will think of you. Thankfully I don't mind taking out my portfolio. There are agents who do this, but I like meeting the people I'm going to work for.'

Among the people to whom Danny feels particularly indebted for passing work his way over the years is the designer Steve Ridgeway of Splash Studio, to whom he was introduced by Ian Hughes of Hodder and Stoughton. They have been associated in a wide variety of jobs and in many ways Ridgeway has filled a vacuum created by leaving college. 'Once college is over there is a possibility of getting a little stale. Because there is no fresh and consistent critical input you can start to wonder if you are developing. Steve Ridgeway has been almost like a college tutor to me – full of ideas and advice and you always know he has your best interest at heart. There are plenty of other illustrators he could have used at times but for some reason he kept putting things my way.'

A personal factor that Danny finds affects his work flow is his relationships with women: 'I don't understand where the perseverance and motivation come from in people who work for and by themselves. I do my best work when I have a partner and life is going smoothly. Then it is easy to relax and keep on top of the paintings in hand plus the hassle of marketing.'

Danny admits that 1989-90 was a bad year for him, partly because a particularly important relationship came to a close then. 'It's hard to concentrate on work when you're desperately trying to think of ways to get your girlfriend back. I coped by making a big effort to change my social pattern – working certain hours a day, playing football again and generally rediscovering habits and hobbies that I had dropped because of being so glad to be living with a wonderful girl. Part-time teaching in evening classes helped and luckily, I had a good gang of friends. Gradually, things picked up. Something inside makes you carry on. It was my first really deep breakup and looking back on it I feel I got off lightly. Through it all I never lost sight of the fact that I'm very lucky to be paid for doing something I enjoy so much – paid to live in a dream world.'

1989-90 was also a period of slight recession in SF publishing and Danny found himself having to look elsewhere for employment. Fortunately, his horror work was in demand and for a while he found himself almost single-handedly providing Victor Gollancz with covers for this field. Doing covers for computer games also proved interesting work, though breaking into the business has been a rather hit and miss affair as the lines of contact remain a slight mystery. Which is a shame because he would like to do more of this work.

In fact, the business of publishing generally remains full of mysteries – such as why one's work can be lapped up by one publisher and totally ignored by another – but Danny takes this as an ongoing challenge.

▶ CYBERNETIC SAMURAI **1987**
GOUACHE AND INK.
9.05 x 13.3 IN. (23 x 34CM).
Cover for a book by Victor Milan, Hodder and Stoughton. The story is about a brilliant lady scientist who creates the first real artificial intelligence into which has been built, presumably as a safeguard, the Bushido code of loyalty. Danny's aim for the cover was to highlight the strange contrast between ancient and modern Japan, all presided over by the eternal Mount Fuji in the distance.

Danny's first love was nature drawing, but the chance to do any professional work in this line did not come along till 1991, and then a touch of deviousness was required to secure the commission.

A problem with illustration (as with no doubt many other professions) is that a reputation in one area not only is no help when trying to branch out into another, it can even be counterproductive. When he heard of a commission for some nature illustration that was going, Danny decided to apply but was advised not to mention his fantasy reputation. So he produced a few sample paintings of birds and insects and submitted them more or less anonymously as if he was fresh from college. The ruse worked and led to him producing a mass of colour illustrations of birds and insects for two volumes in the Nature Detective series published by Franklin Watts.

The work was very satisfying both in itself and because the books are widely used in schools and available in most libraries. Indirectly it also helped enrich his fantasy work by making him look closer at nature than he had done for a while. This is particularly noticeable in some of the paintings he produced specifically for this book, such as those on pages 22 and 28.

Danny's cover was eventually blown when one of the designers involved suddenly recognized his name from years before when she had worked at a different publishers: 'That's not the same Danny Flynn that does all the weird stuff is it?' she bemusedly enquired. But, commented Danny, 'By then I had successfully illustrated the first book so it did not matter. As for the Insects book, some of the specimens shown were more bizarre and alien looking than many of my strangest unearthly creatures. Have you ever seen the caterpillar of a Puss moth, found on Willow trees in the summer, or a Praying Mantis? One of my all-time fears as an illustrator finally came along when the text of the book required a painting of...an earwig. Since childhood I have been terrified of these tiny pincered creatures and it took some serious psyching up to compose myself enough to do the artwork.'

► **OCEANS OF VENUS 1987**
GOUACHE AND INK.
9.05 x 13.3 IN. (23 x 34CM).
Cover for a book by Isaac Asimov, Lightning Books. This book was written at a time when it was believed that Venus had surface water, this theory has since been disproved. This was Danny's first attempt at painting a spaceship and a number of people have commented on its resemblance to Thunderbird 2, but he says any plagiarism was purely unconscious.

◄ **YEARS OF THE CITY 1986**
GOUACHE AND INK.
7.8 x 12.5 IN. (20 x 32CM).
Cover for a book by Frederik Pohl, Hodder and Stoughton. The story is set in a future where New York has been encased in a giant dome. Hang-gliding is illegal there except on the 4th of July, when hang-gliders are allowed to take to the air to burst all the celebration balloons that would otherwise clog up the dome.

The painting took much longer than anticipated, and consequently, Danny had nightmares about getting it finished. The horrible dreams featured a three-legged creature, the colour of old chewing gum, who destroyed Danny's equipment and stamped paint and ink all over the recently finished painting.

◀ **STARSHIP TROOPERS 1986**
GOUACHE AND INK.
11.4 x 15.3 IN. (29 x 39CM).
Cover for a book by Robert Heinlein,
New English Library. Imagery in the
text provided Danny with a perfect
excuse for painting an alien desert
scene that he could fill with shells
and fossils from his collection. He
would be delighted if anyone could
identify the tower-like projection on
the left, it was painted from a fossil
he found on a Greek beach.

◄ **MOONS OF JUPITER 1987**
GOUACHE AND INK.
9.05 x 13.3 IN. (23 x 34CM).
Cover for a book by Isaac Asimov,
Lightning Books. Danny clearly
remembers the night he put the
finishing touches to this picture. It
seemed rather windy, with twigs
tapping at the window. However, only
when he tried to deliver it the next
day did he learn that he had worked
through the worst hurricane in living
memory and that the main road from
Oxford to London was completely
impassable.

► **UTOPIA I BORDER 1990**
GOUACHE AND INK.
16.5 x 23.6 IN. (42 x 60CM).
Computer game box cover, Gremlin
Graphics. To create three-
dimensional displays the publishers
wanted this illustration in two parts,
a border and background which were
then combined to form a single
image for the box cover.

▲ UTOPIA I 1990

GOUACHE AND INK.

16.5 x 23.6 IN. (42 x 60CM).

Computer game box cover, Gremlin Graphics. The aim of this game is to create a perfect environment. As much as he enjoys computer games, Danny is a bit wary of them having been totally addicted to *Space Invaders* after its appearance in 1979. Much to his chagrin he could never beat his brother at this, but later got his revenge with one of its successors, *Astrofighter*. Recently, he came across an old *Astrofighter* game in an arcade, 'It felt brilliant playing it again. Funnily enough I hadn't forgotten any of the moves.'

▶ UTOPIA II 1991

GOUACHE AND INK.

16.5 x 23.6 IN. (42 x 60CM).

Computer game box cover, Gremlin Graphics. Although printed with a different border, the requirement was for the same scene as the previous painting, only not at war. Restoring the city to a state of wholeness made Danny feel rather like a builder. The game was one of the top-sellers of that year.

▲ MOONFALL **1991**
GOUACHE AND INK.
16.5 x 23.6 IN. (40 x 60CM).
Computer game box cover, Hewson
Games. The game was based on a
scenario of ET-like aliens building a
base on the moon from where they
hoped to conquer Earth. Although it
meant the work would take longer,
Danny decided to try a larger format
than usual for this commission.
Then, halfway through the painting,
the completion deadline was
brought forward.

▶ PARADROID **1990**
GOUACHE AND INK.
16.5 x 23.6 IN. (40 x 60CM).
Computer game box cover,
Hewson Games.

CHAPTER FIVE

OTHER WORLDS

CORAL SHORELINE 1990
GOUACHE AND INK.
17.3 x 22.8 IN. (44 x 58CM).
Private work. Danny produced this piece
as a sample painting, a kind of calling
card to show art directors the kind of
work he is capable of and most
interested in doing.

IN THE SUMMER OF 1992, by the time he had completed illustrating the
Insects book for Franklin Watts, Danny felt out of touch with
Science Fiction and recognized the need to send samples of his
work to his various contacts again, since many of them may have
assumed he had given up.

Then at the end of June he received a phone call out of the blue
one evening: 'Hello, is that Danny Flynn? I've been trying to track you
down for ages, this is Frederick Clarke.'

Assuming the call was something to do with unpaid poll tax,
Danny rather wished he hadn't picked up the phone. However, it
turned out that Frederick was the brother and agent, famous in his
own right in publishing circles, of the legendary Arthur C. Clarke in
whose honour a 75th birthday celebration was being planned. It was
to take place in Minehead, the town of his birth. On the strength of
his cover illustration for *Expedition to Earth* six years earlier, a
favourite with both Clarkes, Danny was asked to set up an exhibition
at the festival.

His reaction may be imagined. The timing alone was enough to
make him want to dance around the room. Why this particular picture should have attracted such attention Danny finds it hard to say:
'You hope to make every picture a masterpiece, but you can never
really tell what other people will like.'

With only a week in hand, twenty paintings had to be framed in
a hurry and then he headed for Devon, his first visit to the West
Country. The Minehead Space Festival was due to last for a week so
to help pass the time Danny decided to do a 1992 version of the original EXPEDITION picture. By working on it day and night he managed
to complete it in the available time and visitors returned occasionally
to see how it was progressing.

The highlight of the week was meeting the guest of honour himself. He let his brother do most of the talking as he leafed through
Danny's portfolio but was, says the artist: 'Ever so pleasant, as nice a
man as you could ever hope to meet.'

Such recognition was very flattering and afterwards Danny felt
ready to take on the world. He has remained in regular contact with
Frederick Clarke since, who is a great enthusiast for anything to do
with fantasy or science, and the picture he painted in Minehead is due
to hang in the town's museum and is dedicated to the town's famous
literary son.

Danny has also shown his work elsewhere. A couple of years ago
in Oxford he had an exhibition which, helped by a mention on the
radio and Central Television News, was packed out by adults and
children alike. This led Danny to ponder anew the question of how
long it will be before established art galleries recognize that fantasy
illustrators not only offer a vast range of styles and skills but can also
generate enormous interest. However, he does not really expect the
answer to be soon. At college he took part in many arguments about
the relative merits of fine art and illustration which raged deep into
the night without ever, as far as he can remember, reaching a conclusion (though this may have had something to do with the alcohol
that fuelled these discussions).

Some reactions to the Oxford exhibition were amusing. Many
people said they 'never realized people did this kind of thing', as if
fantasy pictures were somehow mechanically generated. Others
expressed surprise that Danny was such an easy-going, friendly person considering the bizarre nature of most of his work.

'Where do your ideas come from?' This was the most common
question asked at the exhibition, and one often faced by fantasy
artists. Danny comments, 'Non-artists often find it hard to grasp the
idea that these paintings are usually the result of careful planning and

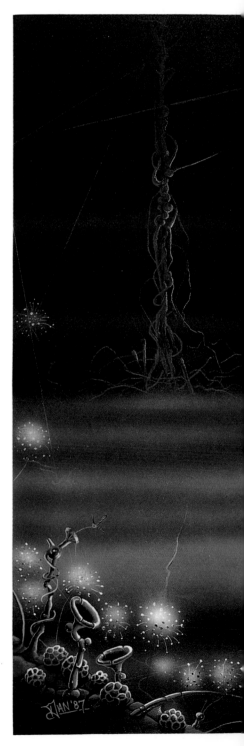

▼ **BETWEEN PLANETS 1986**

GOUACHE AND INK. 10.2 x 14.9 IN. (26 x 38CM).
Cover for a book by Robert Heinlein, Hodder and Stoughton. According to the
text, if you are ever on Venus and find yourself walking through a murky
swamp there is a good chance that one or several mud lice will have attached
themselves to your legs. This parent and offspring appear to be pondering the
deeper meaning of their miserable existence.

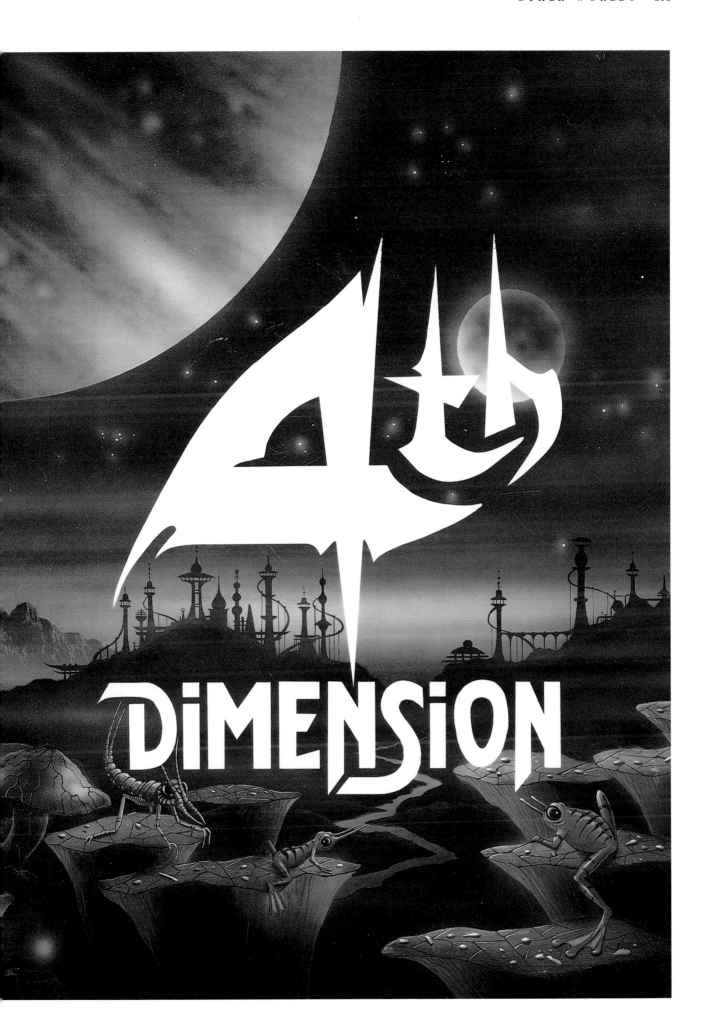

forethought; and usually a creative response to a paragraph of text. Often people imagine they have miraculously materialized after taking some mind-expanding drugs or vast quantities of alcohol. Since a very steady hand is required for the finer details of a painting, a Guinness session would be fairly pointless; and as for drugs – I do not even smoke cigarettes and, beyond sampling a few magic mushrooms, have never been remotely interested in dabbling with drugs. I am quite able to think up bizarre creatures and places without any artificial help.'

Around the same time the local newspaper sent a reporter to interview Danny, who happened to bump into him while out walking the dog. Did he know anything, he was asked, about the strange guy up on the hill who painted such weird pictures? Seeing an opening for a practical joke, Danny proceeded to feed him a batch of horrific and scary tales about the eccentric: 'I think he was a little disappointed when he realized the truth, and that I did in fact have only one head and two arms.'

Speaking of aliens, does he believe they really exist? 'As someone said, there are more stars and planets in space than grains of sand on all the beaches of the world. There must be a real chance of extra-terrestrial life. I would like to believe there are friendly aliens as in *Close Encounters*, which to me is the most realistic vision of the possibility yet achieved on film. Some people claim aliens are already here. It would be interesting to see what would happen if humans were faced with an unfriendly lot – whether we would club together and forget our wars and rivalries or just fall apart.'

Often on walks through the farmland around Oxford Danny wonders what he would do if a strange craft descended from the sky. 'Probably I would be as frightened as anyone else. Would I go on board? Possibly, if guaranteed a return plus messages to family and friends. I think we probably all have some belief that leads to accepting the possibility of life from other planets, as shown by the success of the film *E.T.*'

Obviously he is an enthusiast of space travel but not a total one. Occasionally, he feels the human urge to colonize space and ignore the existence of the very many unresolved mysteries here on Earth – riddles of history and human nature such as Stonehenge, the Pyramids, ghosts and psychic powers: 'There is still so much we need to learn about ourselves, such as why we can't love and protect our own world first, before we leap around the heavens damaging other planets. Wouldn't it be great if, just before we die, some angel of wisdom came down to give answers to any such questions we might want to ask?'

Returning to Earth for a bit, there is more to be said about Danny's work methods. The media he uses are mainly gouache paint and Magic Color inks, about which he is so enthusiastic he cannot understand why more artists don't use them. He uses an airbrush for skies and 'atmospheric' areas, but most of the work is executed with very fine brushes. This he finds time-consuming but satisfying, and in fact, he is progressively phasing out the airbrush from his pictures.

Danny is not much of a morning person. If a painting is going well he will often work into the middle of the night when there are no phone calls, friends or open pubs to distract him. For company he has the stereo, often arranging (until recently when it was axed) his work schedule to catch 'whispering' Bob Harris on the BBC, whose late show from midnight to early morning featured a wide range of music. On one occasion when Bob invited people to write in, Danny did so and they struck up quite a friendship: 'It felt weird having Bob Harris chatting to me in the middle of the night when I was otherwise all alone at my drawing board. It was almost possible to believe

◄ **Previous page**
FOURTH DIMENSION 1989
GOUACHE AND INK.
11.9 x 20.4 IN. (30 x 52CM).
Computer games cover, Hewson Games. This picture was for the cover of a compilation of the company's best-selling games, which meant a loose brief and a great excuse for Danny to create an alien environment full of strange and wonderful creatures. The green and purple colour scheme was prompted by a shirt Danny had just bought. One suspects the combination works better in the painting.

► **CAT WHO WALKS THROUGH WALLS 1986**
GOUACHE AND INK.
8.6 x 14.1 IN. (22 x 36CM).
Cover for a book by Robert A. Heinlein, New English Library. Danny was so pleased to be given this commission, the first of many Heinlein covers, that he came up with about nine alternative designs to be sure of having at least one that the publishers would like.

he was tucked away somewhere inside the radio.'

He sent in some samples of his work, and when Harris became a father, Danny sent him the original of a painting he had particularly praised over the airwaves. They have also spoken on the phone and in fact discussed this book, but sadly the show was axed during the book's preparation – a great loss, Danny feels, not only for himself but many other nightbirds and lovers of good music: 'I think the BBC has made a big mistake here and hope they soon change their minds and ask him back.'

Danny's interest in Paper Tiger as a publisher goes back a long way. Back before the company even existed, in fact, if one counts an interest in artists whose collections of work Paper Tiger later published.

In 1973-4 while still at school and buying records such as *Tubular Bells, Dark Side of the Moon* and everything by Alice Cooper and Tangerine Dream ('old hippy me' he comments wryly), he also began collecting *Science Fiction Monthly* magazine, which featured early examples of illustration by Jim Burns and Bruce Pennington. This was the first time he had seen really classy SF illustration and it started him looking closely at book jackets, a habit he retains to this day – current fellow artists he admires including Geoff Taylor, Mike Van Houten and Stephen Bradbury.

Then, as related earlier, he had the almost revelationary experience of acquiring Roger Dean's book *Views*, followed in due course by others featuring the exceptional work of Patrick Woodroffe and Rodney Matthews and, in fact, he has since collected almost every other book Paper Tiger has published. It feels very strange now, he says, that his own time has come; a bit like a fan joining his favourite football team.

Just as strange was finally meeting Roger Dean in the flesh while this book was in the throes of preparation – Dean was in Oxford to promote a new calendar plus the re-issue of his books and some posters. 'It was a little daunting – meeting him amidst that display of so much of my favourite work, but he was very welcoming. I couldn't help but think back to my foundation course in Grimsby. Now, exactly half my lifetime later, I get to meet the man and discuss my own book with him. I wonder, if *Views* hadn't appeared, whether mine would ever have seen the light of day. It felt like the closing of a full circle.'

The closing of a circle, the ending of a chapter, arriving at a crossroads – whichever metaphor one prefers, Danny feels his life is entering a new phase with birthday number thirty-five having trickled by recently.

In many ways he feels his first decade as a freelance illustrator has been one long learning process and artistically he feels sure the best is yet to come. The directions his work may take are hard to predict because so much depends on the openings that arise; but he would, for example, very much like to concentrate for a whole year on illustrating some story of his own – for which he has several options to choose from.

Also, going back in a way to the very beginning – to the Krater Kreechurs that kicked off his fantasy drawing and his own invented characters that followed and which he scattered in his wake around Scunthorpe like a trail of confetti, around school and on beermats and phonepads – he would like the opportunity to develop his own species further. He has in fact a scenario in which creatures with quirky names such as Degzeg, Snizwib, Sgrune Berune and Blafni live out adventures in an exotic space garden inhabited by an assortment of weird flora and fauna, curiosities including Pugdimples, Nubrubbles, Bibbagrunts and Quazburrees. Designing characters for

▶ **THRUSH ON THE MOON 1992**
GOUACHE AND INK.
11.8 x 17.7 IN. (30 x 45 CM).
Private work. This began as an idea for a college project, but until recently it has been stashed away in what Danny calls his 'sketch-book of future pictures to paint when time allows'. He would eventually like to illustrate a whole book of familiar creatures in unlikely settings: 'I love visual surprises, which I think stems back to my teenage enthusiasm for the Surrealists.'

films is also an ideal goal, particularly for the *Star Wars* saga if it is ever rekindled.

As an artist Danny feels there are many areas left to explore. 'In practice there is always a conflict between trying to improve the work you are known for and experimenting just for the fun of it. Because most of my work is so detailed, I occasionally feel a desire to go abstract on giant canvases by way of relief. At the same time I would like to push further against the limits of what I have achieved. Breaking into the American market would be great because their higher fees allow more time to spend on each picture, and time to spend on private projects. Whatever happens, I know I can't escape from the creative journey I have begun, nor do I even want to. Who knows what the next ten years will bring?'

▼ **CLAY'S ARK 1990**
GOUACHE AND INK. 5.9 x 9.8 IN. (15 x 25CM).
Cover for a book by Octavia Butler, Victor Gollancz. The story
tells of an astronaut who returned to Earth long after it has
been presumed his mission had ended in tragedy. However, he
had unwittingly contracted an alien virus, which caused his
children to develop with insect-like speed once they were born,
and to have feline features. An unusual and well-written novel in
Danny's estimation.

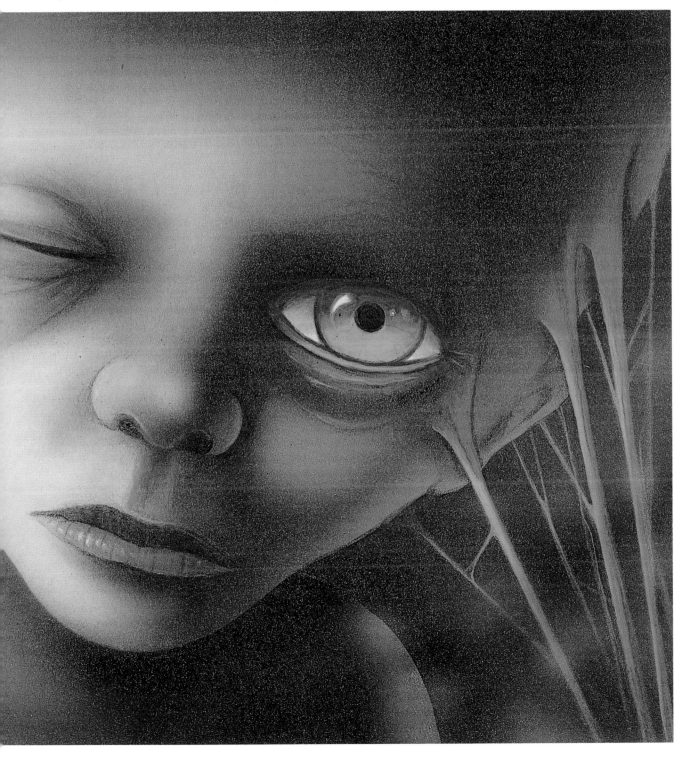

▼ MIND OF MY MIND **1990**
GOUACHE AND INK. 5.9 x 10.2 IN. (15 x 26CM).
Cover for a book by Octavia Butler, Victor Gollancz.
Visualizing a single image that gives an accurate feel of the
whole story is often quite difficult. Even though the
publishers liked what Danny came up with in this case, he
did not personally feel it did the book justice.

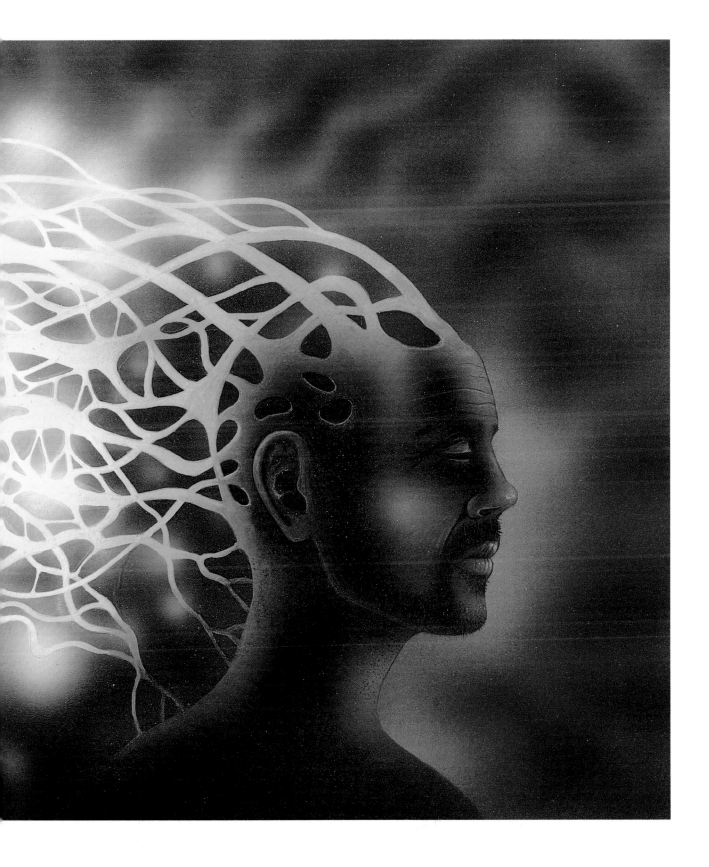

◀ **EXPEDITION TO EARTH 1986**
GOUACHE AND INK.
11.8 x 18.8 IN. (30 x 48CM).
Cover for an anthology by Arthur C.
Clarke, New English Library. Danny
still clearly remembers first reading
this book one night shift while
working for British Steel. So imagine
his excitement some six years later
when he was commissioned to re-
jacket this collection of short stories,
and the still greater excitement of
learning after a further six years that
it is one of the author's favourite
illustrations.

   As with all book jacket
illustrations, the art director needs
to see a rough visual first (see top
left). Even though it is a scribbly
sketch it may have taken many
hours. However, the idea for this one
came instantly, depicting the kind of
creature that may be around long
after humanity has disappeared.

▼ STARMAKER **1987**

GOUACHE AND INK. 10.2 x 12.5 IN. (26 x 32CM).
Cover for a book by Olaf Stapleton, Penguin
Books. According to Danny, 'This is a great and
profound book full of so many incredible alien
beings and cultures that almost every paragraph
is potential cover material. The only SF I've read
in recent years which describes aliens so well is
Master of Paxwax by Philip Mann, it's a shame
there isn't more of this kind of writing around at
present.'

▼ **RED PLANET 1989**
GOUACHE AND INK. 12.5 x 18.1 IN. (32 x 46CM).
Cover for a book by Robert Heinlein, Victor Gollancz. The sunflower in this picture was prompted by the sale of a Van Gogh sunflower painting that week for a cool £26 million. Danny is open to offers.

▲ **PUPPET MASTERS 1987**

GOUACHE AND INK. 8.6 x 12.5 IN. (22 x 32CM).

Cover for a book by Robert Heinlein, New English Library. The
slug-like aliens in this book invade Earth and believe they're going
to take over. Once they've firmly attached themselves to your
shoulders you belong to them – mind, body and soul. The
challenge for Danny, 'was to make them disgustingly believable,
but unlike anything found on this planet.'

▲ I WILL FEAR NO EVIL **1987**
GOUACHE AND INK. 2.2 x 17.7 IN. (31 x 45CM).
Cover for a book by Robert Heinlein, New English Library. The story tells
of a man's mind transplanted into a woman's body – masculine desires
wrapped in feminine appeal. Danny's girlfriend at the time had wanted
to feature in one of his book covers for a while and this was her
chance.

   In general, though, Danny is reluctant to paint the main character of a
story large on the front cover, preferring to let readers do the visualizing
themselves. Unless, of course, the main characters are aliens.

▼ **DINOSAURS 1993**
GOUACHE AND INK. 9.8 x 13.7 IN. (25 x 35CM).
Personal work. As well as being famous for its
sportsmen such as Kevin Keegan, Tony Jacklin
and Ian Botham, Scunthorpe is known for its
many interesting fossil discoveries. Here
Danny tried to imagine how it may have looked
long before the steelmills sprang up,
themselves doomed to become industrial
dinosaurs.

▶ **JOURNEY TO THE CENTRE 1988**
GOUACHE AND INK.
8.2 x 12.5 IN. (21 x 32CM).
Cover for a book by Brian Stableford,
Hodder and Stoughton. The first of
an enjoyable trilogy packed with
many weird and wonderful aliens
including this one – a particularly
unpleasant character called Heleb, a
Spirellian.

▼ **THE MAN WHO SOLD THE MOON 1987**
GOUACHE AND INK.
8.6 x 12.9 IN. (22 x 33CM).
Cover for a book by Robert Heinlein, New English Library. These creatures first appeared in a painting for Danny's major college project. He was delighted to get the chance to paint them again professionally, on their own and with a fresh setting and colour scheme.

▶ **HOTHOUSE 1993**
GOUACHE AND INK. 10.6 x 14.1 IN. (27 x 36CM).
Private work. The inspiration for this painting came from one of the many books Danny read in his three years at British Steel. This one by Brian Aldiss was his clear favourite – a fascinating tale about the adventures of some creatures in the dangerously unpredictable jungle of their planet. The reader is made to feel that at any moment something could drop out of the sky and kill off a favourite character. The illustration does not show any specific image from the story, but aims to capture the general feel.

▶ **SWAMP CREATURE 1988**
GOUACHE AND INK.
5.5 x 7.2 IN. (14 x 18.5CM).
Private work. Danny calls this little
fellow a Zicnoof, and it makes
occasional cameo appearances
scrabbling around the undergrowth of
certain book jackets. 'I'm currently
working on a project about a bizarre
space garden with other creatures
just as strange in it.'

▶▶ **HUNTER OF WORLDS 1989**
GOUACHE AND INK.
9.05 x 13.3 IN. (23 x 34CM).
Cover for a book by C.J. Cherryh,
Mandarin Books. A close rendition
of the author's description of this
female, down to her unusual
jewellery and the 'whites' of her
eyes being blue.

▼ **FARMER IN THE SKY 1990**
GOUACHE AND INK.
11.8 x 17.7 IN. (30 x 45CM)
Cover for a book by Robert Heinlein,
Victor Gollancz. The tale of an
attempt to colonize one of Jupiter's
moons. Danny used the apple tree in
his garden and a friend's cows as
models.

CHAPTER SIX

TACKLING A COMMISSION

DARK STAR I 1993
GOUACHE AND INK.
7.4 x 9.4 IN. (19 x 24CM).
Bottle label for TNT Cider.

TACKLING A COMMISSION 125

▲ TNT Dark Star and TNT Liquid Dynamite promotional flyers.

◄ No these are not the tripods from *War of the Worlds*, but are in fact carbon fibre display stands to house both TNT bottles.

Overleaf
DARK STAR II 1993
ACRYLIC PAINT.
22.8 x 28.3 IN. (58 x 72CM).
Promotional poster and box packaging for TNT Cider.

▼ TNT Dark Star backdrop as prepared for the product launch at a trade show in Manchester.

'THE THING ABOUT FREELANCE ILLUSTRATION' says Danny, 'is you never know what you're going to get to do next. Sometimes I do wish the job was more secure, but also I am not suited to mixing with the same people at work every day and knowing more or less what I'm going to do. There are always surprises in freelancing, as in this case with Dark Star cider. The job just came out of the blue.'

What happened was that after a busy day in London Danny stopped off at an Oxford pub for a quiet pint and a bite to eat, only to be introduced by the landlord to a businessman who was on the lookout for someone to paint a space scene. He did not look like a businessman, being dressed in a teeshirt and jeans. He looked anything but, in fact, but over a few beers it turned out the man was co-director of a beer-importing company that was expanding into developing new products. Under the brand name of TNT they had already marketed a strong white cider in a uniquely shaped bottle with an all-over label that made it resemble a stick of dynamite. Now they wanted an image for a companion brew called Dark Star.

A meeting was arranged at which it transpired that the company's Directors, Adrian and Mark Round, were identical twins whom Danny still cannot tell apart unless one happens to grow his hair. Apart from this slight confusion they hit it off well and Danny's portfolio proved to be just what they were looking for, particularly his Asimov covers.

'For me the attraction was that it was something different to get into – an interesting challenge. In SF illustration you are usually limited by the cover format whether it is books, computer games or whatever, so it was refreshing to try something different. Also, I thought it a bold venture, a very non-traditional approach to marketing, which was exciting to be involved in.'

For the image he was given a fairly free hand because his clients did not have a specific idea of what they wanted, beyond it having a spacey feel and an overall format that echoed their stick of dynamite. Also the design needed to look good on a cylindrical bottle, should stand out on a shelf of other bottles and look interesting from whatever angle it was viewed (on the assumption that not all bar staff would line the bottles up neatly facing forward).

Within these constraints Danny set to work and came up with a variety of ideas which were kicked around at meetings in the Blue Boar inn at Longworth, one of Danny's favourite pubs. From these sessions emerged the idea of having a bright star to echo the igniting spark on the corresponding Liquid Dynamite label, a moon catching the light of this star, a Jupiter-like planet in the background and the brand name picked out in asteroids that trailed off around the back of the bottle. These basic elements remained constant to the end, subject only to modification.

When a mock-up emerged it was tried out immediately on the pub clientele, which led to slight changes of colour and design, such as shifting a few boulders here and there. Then once they felt close to a final design a few samples were made up and tried in pubs all over the Oxford area, which led to further slight modifications.

Danny enjoyed this way of working and admired both the boldness and informality of the enterprise. 'Most companies in the same position would bring in some market research experts but the Round brothers prefer to do their own, relying on the honest opinions of those they approached to hold true for the wider world. Some market researchers would no doubt dismiss this as an amateurish method but, as the launch of their first new cider was deemed by the *Off Licence News* to be the "UK's most successful cider launch ever," there must be something about it that works.'

So far so good. Danny came up with a design for the bottle that everyone was happy with, then by reproportioning it he produced a promotional poster and packaging label. Then he thought he could relax but the third and most strenuous task lay in wait for him.

With little warning he was asked also to produce the backdrop for the company stand at a vital trade fair – an enlargement of the design on to a screen thirty-six feet (11 metres) long by eight feet (two and a half metres) high. Never having worked on such a scale before, he was thrown into a mild panic – but of course he felt too many people were relying on him to quibble.

The materials employed were acrylic paint on a length of hot-air balloon material. This was stretched out and pinned to the floor for the scaled-up design to be drawn on to it, in which there were various incidental complications, such as a giant pair of compasses having to be made for drawing the outline of the large planet. This all took place in a large, disused warehouse and with it came further hazards for Danny, such as the stencils peeling apart in the dampness of the place, and the fact that it was home to a throng of starlings. Not least of the stresses arose from the stream of spectators muttering variations on a theme of: 'He'll never be finished in time.' The only people not panicking appeared to be the Round brothers and this in its way was almost as disconcerting.

However, Danny knew there was no point trying to rush this stage and in due course (over halfway through the week) the backdrop was ready to be fixed up on to a wall and attacked with the airbrush and large hand brushes, with which Mark Round helped.

Was it finished in time? Of course, though Danny was left suffering from severe sleep deprivation and overdoses of Deep Heat and painkiller taken to counter a cricked neck sustained in the middle of the job.

Danny: 'Thankfully "emergency jobs" like these are not too common, but it is amazing what you can achieve when stretched to the limit. It was a good experience to look back on and a great comfort to know it was well appreciated. It was the most talked about stand at the show and once you start getting the compliments back the effort feels worthwhile. One of the key factors is not even allowing yourself to think of the possibility of failure.'

ACKNOWLEDGEMENTS

THE ARTIST WOULD LIKE TO THANK the following people for their encouragement, creative help and work put his way over the years: Mrs K. McCowan, Graham Wells, Charles Potts, John Hall, Brian Love, Harry Willock, Colin Wilcox, Philippa Dickinson, Steve Lang, Dennis Barker, Ian Hughes, Dave Grogan, Faith Brooker, Steve and Julie Ridgeway, Ian Stewart, Andrew Hewson, James Neffendorf, Rob Fisher, Sarah Ridley, Frederick Clarke, Richard Corfield, Mark and Adrian Round; Pippa Rubinstein and everyone at Dragon's World, especially Nigel Suckling for the text.

.... and these friends for more general support: Anne and Mike Hills, Marie Carter, Mr Gerry Lowe, Nick Hardy, Sam and Iris Seeley, Pete and Trish Wallace, Yvette Franklin, Lynn Tune, Mr and Mrs Bill Patterson, Paul Gaskin and Craig, Andy Richmond, Vanessa and Martin Watson, Jane Buttrick, Andrew Forrest, Dave Watson, Debbie Hinks, Paul Finn, Pete Hudspith, Paul Reeson, Bill Galloway, Barry Scutt, Alison Leslie, Mr and Mrs Geoff Barnett, Adam Barnett, Gary Hall, Sarah Lamb, Mr and Mrs Gordon Roache, Tony Griffin, Julia Morrison, Jo de Goris, Stuart Haigh, Galal Mansour, Barrie McDowell and Tess, Carlton Simmonds and Sylvie Greget.

The artist would like to acknowledge that the concept for THE OCEAN on page 6 came from an original idea by Steve Coleman.